Transatlantic Economic Relations in the Post–Cold War Era

BARRY EICHENGREEN

Editor

A Council on Foreign Relations Book

The Council on Foreign Relations, Inc., a nonprofit, nonpartisan national membership organization founded in 1921, is dedicated to promoting understanding of international affairs through the free and civil exchange of ideas. The Council's members are dedicated to the belief that America's peace and prosperity are firmly linked to that of the world. From this flows the mission of the Council: to foster America's understanding of its fellow members of the international community, near and far, their peoples, cultures, histories, hopes, quarrels, and ambitions; and thus to serve, protect, and advance America's own global interests through study and debate, private and public.

THE COUNCIL TAKES NO INSTITUTIONAL POSITION ON POLICY ISSUES AND HAS NO AFFILIATION WITH THE U.S. GOVERNMENT. ALL STATEMENTS OF FACT AND EXPRESSIONS OF OPINION CONTAINED IN ALL ITS PUBLICATIONS ARE THE SOLE RESPONSIBILITY OF THE AUTHOR OR AUTHORS.

Council on Foreign Relations Books are distributed by Brookings Institution Press (1-800-275-1447). For further information on Council publications, please write the Council on Foreign Relations, 58 East 68th Street, New York, NY 10021, or call the Director of Communications at 212-434-9400. Or visit our website, www.foreignrelations.org.

Library of Congress Cataloging-in-Publication Data

Transatlantic economic relations in the post-cold war era / edited by Barry Eichengreen.
　　p.　cm.
　　Includes bibliographical references
　　ISBN 0-87609-210-5 (pbk.)
　　1. United States—Foreign economic relations—European Union countries. 2. European Union countries—Foreign economic relations—United States. 3. Monetary policy—European Union countries. 4. Migration, Internal—European Union countries. 5. European Union countries—Emigration and immigration—Government policy. I. Eichengreen, Barry J.
　　HF1456.5.E8 T73 1998
　　337.4073—ddc21

98-8969
CIP

9 8 7 6 5 4 3 2 1

Composition by Linda Humphrey
Arlington, Virginia

Printed by Kirby Lithographic
Arlington, Virginia

Foreword

In the past, economic disagreements between the United States and Europe were given second billing in the interest of maintaining the broad strategic partnership. Now that the strategic imperative is gone, economic issues have assumed a higher profile. This book provides a timely examination of the balance emerging between competition and cooperation in transatlantic economic relations.

The authors ask and try to answer difficult questions: Will either Europe (with its unemployment) or the United States (with its income inequality) modify its own economic model? Is a transatlantic free trade area possible or even desirable? How will the euro affect the global monetary system? By addressing these new transatlantic issues, and their global implications, this book provides a fresh perspective on an enduring partnership.

Gary Hufbauer
Maurice R. Greenberg Chair, Director of Studies
Council on Foreign Relations

Acknowledgments

The authors and editor are indebted to a number of individuals and organizations for their help in shaping the form and content of this book. This volume emerged as the product of the W. Averell Harriman Study Group on Transatlantic Relations at the Council on Foreign Relations. I would like to thank the participants in the study group; its research director, Charles Kupchan; and its chairman, Roger Altman. Alessandra Casella of Columbia University and Morris Goldstein of the Institute of International Economics provided insightful comments at an early meeting of authors. At the production stage, assistance was provided by Delphine Park at the Council on Foreign Relations; Kira Reoutt at the University of California, Berkeley; Rosalind Oliver at the International Monetary Fund; and Nancy Davidson at the Brookings Institution Press. We are grateful to them all.

Barry Eichengreen
Berkeley, California, and Washington, D.C.
March 1998

Contents

Transatlantic Economic Relations in the Post–Cold War Era

Chapter 1

Introduction

Barry Eichengreen

Economic globalization in the aftermath of the cold war may be causing tariffs, capital controls, and transport costs to decline, but it is also putting firms in the United States and Europe in closer competition. With the growth of cross-border banking, securities trading, and other international capital flows, these firms see U.S. and European financial markets as less economically distinct. Policies on one side of the Atlantic—be they central bank decisions over the interest rate, congressional and parliamentary decisions about the budget, or government decisions about competition and regulatory policy—are having strong repercussions on the other. The scope for conflict in such an environment is considerable.

U.S. producers and policymakers are already complaining about Europe's farm subsidies and food product standards (such as restrictions on hormone-treated meat). For their part, Europeans object to U.S. restrictions on trade and investment in the financial, telecommunications, and transport sectors. U.S. antitrust authorities deciding whether to let Boeing and McDonnell-Douglas merge seem little concerned about the implications for the competitive position of Airbus Industrie. In debating whether to form a monetary union, the member states of the European Union have paid little attention to the possible effects on the reserve currency status and exchange rate of the dollar.

To be sure, policymakers on both sides of the Atlantic continue to work toward common goals. Even while pursuing regional initiatives (ratification of the North American Free Trade Agreement, enlargement and deepening of the European Union), U.S. and European governments are pressing for expansion and liberalization of the multilateral trading system. It was their bilateral support that ultimately pushed the Uruguay Round of GATT negotiations to its successful

1

conclusion. And both sides support one another's efforts to secure improved access to markets in Japan and the developing countries. They collaborate through the Group of Ten and the Bank for International Settlements to limit instability in financial markets. They work through the World Bank and International Monetary Fund (IMF) to promote stabilization and liberalization in transforming economies around the world.

This transatlantic economic relationship is the subject of the following chapters. The authors—who are from both the United States and Europe—ask whether the trend in the coming years will be toward conflict or cooperation. Will policymakers be encouraged by their mutual interests to collaborate in the pursuit of common goals? Or will competition generate conflict and recrimination, especially now that the cold war has ended and their common enemy has disappeared?

The discussion opens in chapter 2 with David Soskice's criticism of the pessimistic view that the transatlantic relationship is a fierce race in which deregulatory trends in the United States are forcing European countries to cut wages and benefits, abolish training and apprenticeship schemes, and more generally dismantle social protection in order to meet "cut-rate" American competition. The European tradition of relationship banking, in which banks and firms establish long-term connections around a range of financial services, is not crumbling, Soskice says. Nor are U.S. financial institutions skimming off the financial cream and opening the door to U.S.-style income inequality. Such a gloomy perspective, predicated on the notion that the United States and societies of Western Europe basically disagree on how their political economies should be organized, implies that market access should be restricted and thus does not bode well for the transatlantic relationship.

Although Soskice acknowledges that the political economies on both sides of the Atlantic have evolved along different lines—with European societies supporting collective values through networks and institutions of social regulation and the United States emphasizing individualism and market orientation—this does not mean that a serious conflict is in the offing. Rather, these different value systems—given concrete reality by government policy, private sector action, and historical inheritance—have produced distinct forms of economic organization that encompass financial organization, institutions of education and vocational training, industrial-relations systems, and mechanisms for the transfer of technology.

In most Northern European countries, Soskice notes, large enterprises collectively contribute to elaborate systems of apprenticeship and vocational training. But the vocational and professional skills workers obtain have only narrow application. Furthermore, unions, employers' associations, and governments discourage firms from poaching workers trained by their competitors (since poaching erodes the incentive for firms to underwrite skill formation), while firms provide the long-term commitment to employment necessary to persuade trainees to invest in improving their skills. In the United States, jobs are less secure, no such collective responsibility is acknowledged (even if it were, mechanisms for enforcing it would be lacking), and employers do not underwrite comparable levels of vocational training. The knowledge conveyed by institutions of public education tends to be more general. On the financial front, Europe's bank-based systems allow managers to adopt long-term horizons useful for strategic planning but are miserly with finance for start-ups. America's market-based financial system is generous with venture capital, but the tyranny of the stock market all too often prevents management from seeing beyond the next quarterly profit statement.

Thus there may in fact be no race toward a common model. According to Soskice, U.S. and European institutions each have a comparative advantage. In the United States it resides in new industries with rapidly changing technologies, which can best be exploited through organizational flexibility. In Europe it lies in tailoring goods to the market and in incremental product and process innovation, which rely on a stable labor force and long-term customer relations. Both the American and European forms of economic organization can survive and prosper because markets exist not only for radically new products (such as those based on the electronic and biochemical technologies of Silicon Valley and San Diego) but also for established products whose economic viability is sustained by incremental change (such as the quality machine tools of southern Germany and the fashion textiles of northern Italy).

Openness, says Soskice, can reinforce the viability of this institutional diversity by increasing the gains from specialization. The U.S. and European economies can specialize in producing what they produce best without regard to the constraints of domestic demand. In negotiating a Transatlantic Free Trade Area (TAFTA), for example, there is no need for U.S. policymakers to insist that Europe adopt a uniform deregulated economic system along U.S. lines, or for Europeans to expect their levels of social protection to be replicated in the United States. The two systems can flourish in competition with one another. And the more open the competition, the stronger the gains from institutional diversity. But U.S. pressure for changes in European competition policy, corporate governance, and labor relations could threaten the viability of the European model. Whether further transatlantic integration engenders conflict will depend, therefore, on the particular form it takes.

Relations between the two sides, as Jeffrey Schott points out in chapter 3, are particularly important in matters of trade. Together, the United States and European Union account for more than half of global imports and exports. Although conflicts over industrial policy and agricultural subsidies have festered for years, the United States and the countries of Europe have worked in surprising harmony for the expansion of the multilateral trading system. They have used the General Agreement on Tariffs and Trade (GATT) and the World Trade Organization (WTO) to defuse conflicts that have proven intractable in bilateral negotiations.

But with the end of the cold war and the rise of regionalism, Schott points out, there is new reason to worry about the stability of the bilateral relationship. The United States and the European Union no longer have a powerful incentive, in the form of a common enemy, to paper over their commercial differences. Regional security concerns on their respective doorsteps (in the U.S. case, to the south; in the European case, to the east) are replacing the global goals once pursued in multilateral fora. Some observers are urging the two sides to enter into a TAFTA for this very reason, that is, to refocus attention on the transatlantic relationship.

In Schott's view, a TAFTA is not necessarily the best way to address bilateral trade tensions. U.S. complaints about European policies toward agriculture, intellectual property rights, standards, certification requirements, financial services, and investment all fall within the purview of the WTO. The same is true of EU complaints about U.S. restrictions on trade and investment in financial, telecommunications, and transport services and environmental policies. It would make more sense, he argues, for the United States and Europe to invest in strengthening the WTO than to create a separate venue for bilateral negotiations. Bilateral consultations through the Transatlantic Business Dialogue, among other channels, can contribute to this process, but only if they do not detract from investment in and compliance with WTO rules and procedures.

In chapter 4 Barry Eichengreen and Fabio Ghironi shift the focus from trade to monetary relations. Transatlantic collaboration has been less systematic here than in trade, and institutional flux has been more pronounced. Europe is now completing the transition to monetary unification. Two consequences of this move, argue Eichengreen and Ghironi, may limit policy coordination.

First, the institutions of international monetary cooperation will inevitably be disturbed. Group of Seven (G-7) summits will be complicated when responsibility for the monetary policies of France, Germany, and Italy is assumed by an institution that also determines interest rates for Austria, Ireland, Spain, Portugal, Finland, and the Benelux countries (which are not G-7 members). The IMF will have to consider organizing parallel Article IV consultations with the Euro zone and each EU member state. Institutional relations between Europe's fiscal and monetary authorities will grow increasingly uncertain, thereby complicating cooperative initiatives that require adjustments of both fiscal and monetary policies.

Second, the creation of the European Central Bank (ECB) and a single European currency may put an end to the present international consensus on ways to respond to financial disturbances. Once Europe has a single market and achieves monetary union, it will become more of a large, closed economy and be less preoccupied with exchange rates and exchange rate policy. As long as the ECB is preoccupied with price stability, it will not be inclined to participate in U.S.-led initiatives for concerted intervention in the foreign exchange market. Under the Maastricht Treaty, its lender-of-last-resort responsibilities are ambiguous, and it may hesitate to participate in European lender-of-last-resort operations if these threaten to conflict with its responsibility for price stability. It may be reluctant to contribute to international lender-of-last-resort initiatives for distant countries such as Mexico and Thailand. In the past, Europe entered into international monetary cooperation with the United States and Japan only in periods of serious dislocation (as when the dollar soared in the mid-1980s and slumped in 1994) and during exceptional crises (such as the Mexican meltdown of 1995 and the Asian crisis of 1997). There is a danger, Eichengreen and Ghironi conclude, that even such limited initiatives will prove difficult to arrange in the initial years of Europe's monetary union.

Another issue of growing economic concern in both the United States and Europe is migration. The question here, says Riccardo Faini in chapter 5, is not how policies on either side affect transatlantic relations but what assistance each can gain from the experience and response of the other. The United States has long had a porous border with the countries to its south, whose per capita incomes are a tenth or less of U.S. levels. In contrast, it is only since the collapse of the Iron Curtain and the development of North African expatriate networks that Europe has also had to deal with this issue. Faini uses the experience of the United States as a lens through which to view the impact of immigration on Europe's economy and in the process provides insight into the problem for both sides.

Faini suggests that Europeans, like Americans, are worried about what will happen to the distribution of income if the decline in centralized bargaining allows unskilled immigrants to bid down the wages of unskilled natives. As fiscal limits come to be monitored more closely at the level of the European Union, Europeans will also become preoccupied with the impact of immigration on public finances. The main concern, says Faini, is not so much that the costs of immigration will exceed the benefits, but that foreign workers will become a source of political tension.

Those who wish to limit immigration, whether westward across the Oder or northward across the Rio Grande, can build fences or give migrants an incentive to stay home. These alternatives are not incompatible, argues Faini. Tighter border controls may be the only effective short-term remedy, but incentives for economic development are likely to be the more cost-effective strategy over the long term. Incomes need not be equalized to stem the flow of migrants; even a limited improvement in living standards may be enough to restrain migration by individuals who prefer their established social relationships and local culture. But it takes time for technical assistance, financial aid, and market access to have discernible effects. Enlargement of the North American Free Trade Agreement and the European Union may eventually ameliorate the development problems of

Mexico and Eastern Europe, but, Faini adds, Mexico's crisis of 1994–96 is a clear reminder that economic integration provides no guarantee of immediate policy and political stability, while powerful vested interests may be prepared to slow the European Union's expansion to the east.

The picture that emerges from the essays in this volume is one of problems, not of crises that are likely to transform the transatlantic institutional landscape. Whatever change does take place will be incremental rather than revolutionary, although one should hasten to add that the relationship could deteriorate if the problems are ignored. Such an outcome would be as regrettable as it is avoidable.

Chapter 2

Openness and Diversity in Transatlantic Economic Relations

David Soskice

In recent years the United States and the European Union have undertaken several initiatives to promote further liberalization of trade across the Atlantic. Among these efforts are the New Transatlantic Agenda announced at the end of 1995 and the proposed New Transatlantic Marketplace. These developed out of the U.S. administration's Transatlantic Business Dialogue and the European Commission's Transatlantic Economic Space. Perhaps the only initiative to represent a major attempt at institutionalizing economic arrangements between the European Union and the United States, however, is the Transatlantic Free Trade Area.

The idea of such an arrangement was put forward in 1990 by Britain's prime minister Margaret Thatcher, and it was reiterated in 1994 by Canada's premier Jean Chretien. Recently Germany's foreign minister Klaus Kinkel revived the possibility. Because of the different nature of capitalist organization in the United States and in a number of Northern European economies, particularly Germany, the TAFTA proposal raises some institutional questions.

First, one might ask why a Transatlantic Free Trade Area is needed at all (see also chapter 3 on this question). Liberalized trade and capital movements between the member states of the European Union and the United States are already substantial. Moreover, mech-

The chapter benefited from many useful comments to an earlier draft by members of the Trade and Finance Section of the Study Group on Transatlantic Relations. Helpful discussions with Peter Hall, Stewart Wood, and Stephen Woolcock are also gratefully acknowledged.

anisms are available for further improvement, in the form of general multinational agreements and negotiating structures, as well as a framework for ad hoc negotiations between the European Union and the United States when the need is accepted on both sides. Thus the usual economic reasons for developing an institutionalized regional free trade agreement—namely that there are barriers to trade and limited alternative mechanisms for liberalization—do not apply in this case.

The economic case has a further weakness. One basic reason for institutionalizing trading arrangements between individual or groups of countries is that in their absence disputes may get out of hand and escalate into full-scale trade wars. But although skirmishes erupt from time to time, a trade war is not likely to break out across the North Atlantic. In addition, even if there remain areas such as agriculture in which real economic benefits would flow from further liberalization between Europe and the United States, could a TAFTA serve as the facilitating vehicle? If anything, agriculture would likely prevent a TAFTA from coming about. From a political-economic perspective, hammering out treaty-based agreements is costly in terms of negotiating and political resources: in this respect Asia (the Asia-Pacific Economic Cooperation, APEC) and Latin America (NAFTA, FTAA) both rate more highly on the U.S. list of priorities, reflecting the need for treaties with areas in which large gains can be made and in which the possibility of trade wars is to be taken seriously.

Most transatlantic policy initiatives have been motivated by reasons quite removed from the desire to complete a market in this region.[1] In particular, they should be seen in the context of post–cold war security. During the cold war, mutual interests in security ensured a close relationship between the United States and Western Europe. With its end, European politicians have sought other reasons to maintain transatlantic ties. The disarray of European governments in the security and foreign policy areas and the consequent dominance of the United States have reinforced this search.

It can be concluded that the case for a TAFTA is political rather than economic. Though it should not be overdrawn, there is a parallel here with the debates over European monetary union. The German government has pushed hard for a common currency in the

1. Woolcock (1996b). For useful background material, see Woolcock (1991; 1996a).

belief that it would help *political* integration within the European Union. More subtle economic issues have not always been given the attention they might merit. Of course, the political importance attached to monetary union far outweighs that associated with transatlantic trade; despite Kinkel's support, TAFTA does not even represent an agreed position of the German government.

Nevertheless, the question of market liberalization does intersect with institutional issues, especially as they relate to different systems of advanced capitalism. Many economists have come to accept that certain kinds of institutions may have a marked effect on international competitiveness. This is particularly the case for institutions associated with education and training, technology diffusion, the availability of finance, and the cooperation of labor, all of which play a role in company performance. The advanced economies have organized these institutions in quite different ways, depending on their system of capitalism.[2] These various institutional frameworks provide companies different advantages in developing strategies to market their products; success may arise from the nature of their emphasis on employee skills and cooperation, relations with owners, relations with other companies, and so on.

In other words, patterns of trade in both goods and services, particularly the innovation strategies they reflect, might be explained in part by a theory of *comparative institutional advantage.* Just as firms can be said to draw their effectiveness from individual core competencies, so too firms might derive further gain from *national institutional core competencies.* National or regional institutional core competencies clearly exist within the European Union,[3] and in most cases they cannot easily be transferred to or borrowed from other economies. These different institutional environments, in combination with liberalization, have played an important role in making the U.S. and European economic climate more innovative in the past twenty years or so. The debate surrounding the transatlantic relationship would lead to naught if it failed to recognize the combined benefits of increased openness and national institutional diversity.

The fact is that institutional differences across advanced economies remain a powerful force in global markets for goods and services. Ex-

2. Albert (1991); Crouch and Streeck (1995); Hall (forthcoming); Hollingsworth, Schmitter, and Streeck (1994); Soskice (1990); Soskice (forthcoming).
3. On this point, see Porter (1990).

trapolating from the substantial liberalization of these markets initiated two decades ago and the widespread removal of constraints on the mobility of capital, many economists and political scientists predicted that the institutions of various advanced economies would converge. They saw differences eroding among the formal and informal institutions forming the economic framework in which companies, individuals, and owners of capital operate. The central concern of these institutions ranges from corporate governance, industrial relations (both employee participation within the company and collective bargaining), and relations between companies (technology diffusion, standard setting, contract rules, and competition policy) to education and training. Together they constitute the *national institutional framework* of the economy in question.

With the predicted convergence of national institutional frameworks, observers argued, companies would relocate to economies that imposed the fewest constraints on their activities, and this would lead to "regime competition." That is, governments would reduce constraints in order to discourage domestic companies from relocating to foreign soil while encouraging foreign companies to invest in domestic operations. In the resulting atmosphere of equilibrium across political economies, markets would be substantially deregulated. But liberalization has not led to the type of institutional convergence forecast in the 1980s. This state of affairs is all the more surprising within the European Union, since the Single European Act and then Maastricht underwrote not only the free movement of goods and services and capital, but also that of labor. Hence important institutional differences exist within the European Union itself, as well as between the United States and Western Europe.

The American institutional framework can be summed up as one of more or less deregulated markets.[4] Almost all observers who had forecast convergence assumed that it would move in the direction of an American-style deregulated framework. Despite the mobility of labor and capital, only one EU member, the United Kingdom, has an institutional framework in the mid-1990s close to that of the United States.[5]

4. Despite continued regulation in many economic spheres in the United States (for example, the generation and distribution of electric power are still highly regulated), the overall degree is much more limited than in, say, Germany.

5. Ireland comes next (no reference is made to the Southern European economies, which are still institutionally transitional).

The Northern EU member states (and also Norway and Switzerland) are closer to Germany in this regard: business is collectively organized and remains powerful, for it maintains a cooperative independence from government.[6]

The German and Northern European framework is characterized by close long-term ties between companies and banks, cooperative industrial relations, vocationally oriented systems of education and training, and the possibility of close long-term cooperation between companies. Coordinated business plays a central role both formally and informally. By contrast, the deregulated landscape of the two Anglo-Saxon economies shows none of these features. Instead, its financial systems are noted for providing high-risk capital, the lack of constraints on employee relations enables companies to reposition themselves rapidly, the emphasis is on general education and the exceptional innovation it permits, and the open market in corporate governance makes it possible to purchase and dispose of companies at a rapid pace. A strict competition policy impedes close long-term cooperation between companies; indeed, business coordination is weak and unimportant, except sometimes at the political level.

For the most part, these institutional differences have proved remarkably durable over the past two decades of increasing liberalization. While there has been an important movement toward greater flexibility in Northern Europe, most notably in Sweden, business in the region has not been trying to move to an Anglo-Saxon type of deregulated framework; rather, one of its main concerns has been to deter union movements and governments from imposing egalitarian wages or intervening in company decisions about new technology. It has been equally intent on preserving effective employee participation in company affairs, strengthening long-term corporate governance, and reinforcing technological links with related companies.

---

6. This chapter is primarily concerned with the contrast between the U.S.—and U.K.—institutional frameworks, and that of Germany. It will not refer to France or Italy except in passing. Northern Italy is closest to the German camp, although on a formal level the collective organizational capacities of business are less coherent; Regini (1995) provides a good picture. The French institutional framework is different from that of Northern Europe and the Anglo-Saxon economies: in France, the state (still) plays a central institutional role, increasingly intertwined with the leadership of large companies. More than 50 percent of the CEOs of the two hundred largest private companies have a background in, and close connections to, the public service. See Bauer and Bertin-Mourot (1992); Hancke and Soskice (1996).

Sweden can be seen as moving toward a flexible version of the German model. As the next section explains, the institutional differences between the Anglo-Saxon systems, on the one hand, and Northern European systems, on the other, have been at least partly responsible for observed differences in innovation patterns.

Innovation Patterns

Broadly speaking, the Anglo-Saxon economies—that is, those of the United States and the United Kingdom—can be said to have a competitive advantage in the following areas:[7] radical innovation in newly emerging technologies (such as biotechnology and microprocessors); sophisticated internationally competitive services (such as management consultancy, advertising and related media services, international and investment banking, derivatives, tax consultancies, architectural and engineering consultancies, and auctioneering);[8] and large complex systems, especially where the technology is changing rapidly (as it is in telecommunication systems, large entertainment systems, defense systems, large software systems, airline systems, large aircraft production).

In contrast, countries in the Northern European category—notably Germany, Sweden, and Switzerland—excel in incremental innovation in products and processes, where they are often at the leading scientific edge; and in utilizing established technologies, especially machinery, but also chemicals. Their economies are noted for their complex products and production processes, after-sales service, and close long-term customer links.[9] Furthermore, Germany, Sweden, and Switzerland are not noted for developing new industries.[10] Germany, for example, though strong in research, "cannot match the United

7. On the concept of competitive advantage, see Porter (1990).

8. On the author's calculations using Porter's cross-country classification of internationally competitive industries, the following were the numbers of "internationally competitive" service industries: Germany 7, Sweden 9, Switzerland 14, United Kingdom 27, United States 44. (These figures should be treated with caution because no U.K. data exist for some sectors.)

9. The author's calculations from Porter's data give the number of internationally competitive machinery industries as Germany 46, Sweden 28, Switzerland 35, United Kingdom 17, United States 18. (The caveat in note 8 again applies.)

10. New industries in Sweden and Switzerland are discussed in Porter (1990, pp. 351, 353) and (1990, pp. 325, 327), respectively.

States in inventiveness in new industries. Germany is the undisputed leader in improving and upgrading technology in fields in which its industry is established, but there are weaknesses in newer fields such as electronics, biotechnology and new materials."[11]

That the Northern European environment is not friendly to the Anglo-Saxon style of innovation is clear from the behavior of some major German multinationals. Three of the four major German banks—Deutsche Bank, Dresdner, and West LB—have moved their international operations away from Frankfurt and to London; the fourth, Commerzbank, has tried to find an appropriate vehicle to make the same move. Domestic business, with its long-term relationships and high skills throughout the work force, has remained in Germany. But international operations can be organized more easily in London, where it is less difficult to hire and fire mobile and gifted professionals and to reward them as appropriate. Similarly, the three largest chemical companies—BASF, Bayer, and Hoechst—have moved most of their innovative biotechnology operations from Germany to the United States but have kept their mainstream chemicals research, noted for its high value added, in Germany.

These differences in patterns of innovation have a great deal to do with the economics of organization. A company's ability to innovate in a particular way reflects its ability (or the ability of its top management) to solve what are essentially motivational problems. Different types of innovation make different demands on companies in terms of the relationships they must develop with their employees, with companies that help them develop innovations, with potential competitors (who may also be employees or cooperating companies), and with company owners or financiers. Suppose that a NASDAQ-type company is engaged in developing a radically new technology, say, in the field of biochemistry. This company will find it difficult to monitor a small group of researchers working on an innovation. The company will be unable to give the researchers a long-term contract because this area of science is changing so rapidly that new researchers with knowledge of the new areas will have to be brought in to keep innovation on track, and existing researchers will have to be released. Even if it could offer employment security, the company would have to guard against having researchers walk off with incubated projects.

11. Porter (1990, p. 377). On the situation in other countries of this group, see Porter (1990, pp. 351, 327, 507, 527, 530).

In the case of incremental innovation (modification, customization) of high-quality machinery, the company will still have difficulty monitoring engineers, technicians, and skilled manual employees, all of whom need to be able to carry out their work without much supervision. Here company-specific skills are important and make long-term attachments important. Thus the company may wish to promote employment security in exchange for some system of cooperation through peer monitoring. But how do the employees know whether the company really is providing employment security? And how does the company deal with what will be a potentially powerful work force, with a capacity to hold the company back? Furthermore, how, in each of the preceding examples, can owners be persuaded to finance such activities given the existence of considerable inside information?

These are the kinds of problems that different national institutional frameworks may help resolve. Before considering how they do so, it may be useful to classify innovation strategies as they relate to organizational questions. The following classification is based, first, on whether the innovation (or, rather, the general pattern of innovation) can be accomplished with the company's existing work force and established network of collaborating companies.[12] If so, it is described as incremental innovation; if not, it is called radical innovation (table 2-1). Innovations that require a company to bring in new skills (because they could not be acquired by existing employees, for example, in areas where a new technology is changing in unpredictable ways) are said to be radical in relation to the company defined as a network of established relationships. The same innovation might be incremental for other companies. Radical innovations in this sense are favored by the Anglo-Saxon institutional framework since such a framework gives companies considerable freedom in hiring and firing employees, as well as in buying and selling other companies. By contrast, the German institutional framework, which favors long-term cooperative relations, is more consistent with incremental innovation.

Innovation strategies may also be classified according to the way in which activities within the company are organized. Suppose there is little coordination between different groups of researchers (each of

12. Kitschelt (1991).

TABLE 2-1. *Classifying Innovation Patterns*

Innovation pattern	Uncoupled coordination	Tightly coupled coordination	Loosely coupled coordination
Radical	Innovation in newly emergent technologies (e.g., biotech); sophisticated services (e.g., management consultancy); can be found in the United States and United Kingdom	Complex systems, with rapid pace of innovation (telecom systems, large software systems); can be found in the United States and United Kingdom	. . .
Incremental	. . .	Complex systems with established technologies (e.g., satellites, high-speed train systems); can be found in France	High-quality manufacturing, in established technologies (e.g., complex machinery, fine chemicals); can be found in Northern Europe

which is working on a different problem in biotechnology), between different management consultants in the same company, or between advertising executives working on a particular brand in the same agency. This is described as uncoupled (or essentially uncoupled) coordination (of course, researchers may use common services and may rely on one another to obtain random problem-solving information). Alternatively, coupling may be tight. That is, all of the groups in a company may be highly interdependent, as in a large software system or an airline. What one group or individual does must fit precisely with what is going on elsewhere; changes have to be carried out with great speed and initiated from the center. A third case is known as loose coupling. Here, employees or groups need to be coordinated: many operations tie into other operations. But there is some latitude in the nature of the precise links and in the solutions that are reached for particular parts of design and production problems. Where individual employees or groups have expertise in particular areas, and where their solutions to problems require small changes in related areas (for instance, in customizing a machine), the most efficient way to organize work is to decentralize problem solving. This can generate considerable feedback on design within a company. Thus substantial coordination and discussion, as well as actual joint work, are the defining features of loosely coupled work organization, which implies high employee autonomy and high coordination. This is the kind of work that engineers, technicians, and skilled manual employees do in chemicals and engineering in Germany.[13]

Innovation Strategies and Problem Solving

The next question that needs to be raised is what *relational problems* do the different innovation strategies apply to? For the purposes of this discussion, the strategies thus far classified as radical and incremental innovation can also be labeled U.S./U.K. and Northern European strategies, respectively, on the basis of the institutional frameworks that gave rise to them (see table 2-2).

U.S./U.K. Strategies

The first point to make about U.S./U.K. strategies is that they operate most effectively in deregulated labor markets. There are three reasons for this.

First, these strategies encourage "radical" innovation, which means that new people with expertise in new areas may have to be recruited from outside the firm. A large software company, say, may have to bring in a group who have independently developed an innovative program (perhaps for offering financial services on the Internet); a biotech company may suddenly switch to a new product or a new technique and require the help of researchers with the appropriate expertise; or an international investment bank may need to draw on the specialized knowledge of an individual or group in order to develop a new financial instrument. In all these cases, restrictions on hiring and firing must be minimal, and the firm must be free to set rewards at whatever level is required to persuade people to move.

Second, incentives for U.S./U.K. strategies need to be "high-powered." That is to say, they must be contingent on results, in view of the difficulties inherent in long-term contracts. This is particularly

13. Sorge and Warner (1987).

TABLE 2-2. *National Institutional Frameworks*

Rule	U.S./U.K. framework	German framework
Labor market	Deregulated	Works council plus external supervision by unions and employer associations, professional associations (engineers, chemists); coordinated wage-setting across industries
Vocational training	College-based with minimal industry links	Industry-based, run by employer associations and unions and professional associations for engineers and the like; large company input
Financial	Dispersed shareholder system requiring low-cost, public event monitoring; high-powered CEO incentive structures; high-risk financing possible with symmetric uncertainty; open market in corporate governance	Stable shareholder system; "monitoring" of inside information if diffused across other companies via industry "reputation" monitoring; company consensus decision-making possible
Intercompany relations	Strong competition policy; standards set by market competition; industry associations have no sanctioning power	Requirement to compete in export markets, but weak competition rules domestically, as long as market share not too high; industry associations have strong role in consensus-based standard setting; and some governance of company-supplier relations

the case in companies developing radically new technologies. Monitoring is extremely difficult in such circumstances, and the company may have to wait for an innovation to arrive.

Third, the chief executive officer (CEO) must have unilateral control over decisionmaking, as can be seen in tightly coupled systems engaged in rapid innovation. When a computer operating system such as Windows incorporates Internet browsing software, parameters have to be set rapidly, and this can only be done from the center of the system. Or when an airline installs new cabin configurations, it quickly has to adjust many of its operations—from cabin crew practices, reservations, ticketing, sales, and marketing to flight scheduling, maintenance, safety, and finance—and cannot wait for a consensus to be reached before moving ahead with the changes. Such circumstances are not best handled by regulated labor markets that entail a works council with powers of codetermination in important matters.[14]

U.S./U.K. innovation strategies are also most effective in financial markets that allow both high-risk finance and the quick transfer of corporate governance. An innovating company working on a rapidly changing and unpredictable technology needs to have at its immediate disposal new ideas, components, and processes. The most convenient way to acquire them may be to purchase another company that has developed them.[15] Furthermore, keeping corporate governance on the open market forces industry leaders to put shareholder value ahead of their own competencies in deciding where to take new technologies and what modes of organization to use for this purpose.

Northern European Strategies

The incremental or Northern European style of innovation is best suited to established technologies. Unlike radical innovation, incremental strategies call for employees (engineers, technicians, and skilled laborers) with strong skills in specific product and process technologies for what may be a narrow range of high-quality products. For the most part, such skills are acquired through experience. Hence it costs a great deal to replace employees, as it does to monitor them. In addition, because coordination is needed for effective loose coupling, employees can effectively block, or "hold up," management decisions.[16] Since employees play a vital role in incremental innovation, they occupy a powerful position, which forces the company to adopt a consensus-based approach to decisionmaking. Such an approach binds employees and top management in an implicit long-term agreement: top management will avoid strategies that put em-

14. Lehrer (1996).
15. Allen (1993).
16. Oliver Williamson (1985).

ployment security and relative rewards at risk, while employees will work cooperatively and even monitor one another's performance.

If consensus decisionmaking is to work, difficult problems have to be resolved *inside* the company. Employees have to be reassured that their representatives possess sufficient power and information to protect their interests, and that whatever arrangements are agreed upon cannot at some future time be abrogated by new management. At the same time, if these reassurances are effective, and thus employee representatives are in a strong position, management may see in this situation a possibility for the misuse of employee powers. Both sides need to be able to look to external intervention if the other side moves away from the bargain. In circumstances of consensus decisionmaking, employer associations, professional associations (engineers, chemists), and unions must clearly understand the rules of the employee participation game and have the power to intervene when necessary.

As already mentioned, incremental innovation favors certain kinds of skills on the part of the employee and the company. In situations where innovation is quite narrow, employees need substantial training in deep but narrow competencies at the start of their career; an engineer, for example, should devote initial training to gaining intensive knowledge of a particular range of machinery and associated technology. Although such training improves employment prospects in the industry in question, and normally in the company in which some of the training takes place, the prospects are less favorable elsewhere. Thus some credible commitment needs to be given to the trainees, and not just by the company, that the investment in training makes sense. This in turn means that unions, professional associations for engineers, and the like must be fully integrated into the process of curriculum development. There are corresponding problems for the company, as explained later in the chapter.

In these circumstances, the company needs to be certain that its owners are prepared to supply long-term funding, despite potential difficulties in monitoring the investment. These difficulties arise because much of the future value of the investment is contained in the expertise of the employees and in the value of the firm's long-term relations with cooperating companies. Since these factors do not translate into current profitability, a shareholder or lender cannot easily assess their value. In addition, since company decisionmaking needs to be based on consensus, responsibility cannot be shouldered by the CEO, nor will the CEO have unilateral control over the company. Furthermore, it will be difficult for the owners to give the CEO gigantic rewards.

To remain on the leading edge of research and development in an established industry or technology, a firm practicing incremental innovation must cooperate closely with other companies in the same industry. If the transfer of technology is to be effective, research institutes and a number of companies must work together. Hence companies that may compete in the same markets will have to share inside information if they are to make sensible decisions about what areas of research and development to focus on. Cooperation is also essential if they are to develop common standards in the industry, including interface standards.

In addition, incremental innovation demands a substantial knowledge of the capacities, product market strategies, and technology requirements of individual companies. Otherwise, it will be impossible for the company to train its engineers, technicians, and general labor force effectively. Therefore there must be institutions at the industry level that promote and protect the interests of companies. These institutions must be able to sanction wayward companies and also to engage in policymaking. For such institutions to work, companies in the same domestic industry must not compete so intensely that they feel threatened by cooperation.

Institutional Frameworks

As already mentioned, the prominent features of the institutional frameworks in which innovative strategies arise can be broken down into four "systems": the labor market, vocational training, finance, and intercompany relations (see table 2-2). The U.S./U.K. and German systems typify the differences between the principal frameworks under discussion.

In the United States and United Kingdom, labor markets are deregulated. Companies have considerable freedom to hire and fire and to set reward packages. They are free to place unilateral control in the hands of the CEO and thus are not required to set up decisionmaking bodies that include employee representatives. Since the education and training system of these countries is market driven, it does not impede radical innovation. The required skills can be developed most effectively through the market, since skills are changing unpredictably and rapidly, or through in-house courses. The financial system in these two countries is known for its high-risk capital and open markets in corporate governance. The U.S./U.K. institutional framework puts no obstacles in the way of such finance. Furthermore, it encourages strong competition in product markets and does not insist on close long-term relations between companies. All these factors promote radical innovation.

In Germany, these systems are quite different. The labor market operates through consensus decisionmaking and hence the emphasis is on company and employee security. The market is governed by clear legal rules and clear understandings supported by employer associations and unions; external organizations with sanctioning power are thus available to sort out any problems that may arise. These rules and understandings cover employment security and reward setting and offer security to those engaging in long-run relationships in which they may make substantial fixed investments.[17]

Germany's education and training systems are built around the concept that most young people will invest early and seriously in narrowly focused professional or vocational skills. They believe that such investment will greatly enhance their employment and career prospects, albeit in a restricted area, a notion made credible by the professional associations and unions. Employers, too, have their associations, which encourage companies to participate in the training system so as to offer a clear bridge to long-term employment, as well as to the acceptability of skill certificates if employees move.[18]

Another feature of the German framework is long-term finance. In the case of larger companies, this is a result of stable shareholder understandings and delegated monitoring of corporate performance by banks; in the case of smaller ones, it is a result of the system of regional and federal governance of local banks. This system is strengthened by legal rules governing takeovers. In addition, legal provisions protect the access of local banks to low-interest funds, but they also require banks to consider the local economy in their lending practices.[19]

The great problem for banks in Germany is that they cannot

17. Turner (1991); Berghahn and Detlev (1987).
18. OECD (1994); Soskice (1994); Streeck and others (1987).
19. Franks and Mayer (1990); Vitols (1995).

develop the expertise needed to assess the performance of companies with highly advanced products and technologies. Hence they must rely more on the word of other companies and research institutes than on their own direct monitoring. This situation again calls for substantial cooperation between companies within German industries, which would indeed be difficult in an atmosphere of intense competition over prices or new surprise products. It also suggests that banks can only assess innovations that do not depart too far from established technologies.

In addition, the necessary institutional framework governing the transfer of technology, setting of standards, and direct relations between companies is supported by well-organized business associations acting together with the professional associations.[20] Competition policy does not stand in the way of these activities, either directly, by ruling them illegal, or indirectly, by requiring sharp competition between companies in the same industry.[21] Instead of head-on competition, there is well-established product differentiation. The norms of weak competition prevail only in the domestic market; companies are required to prove themselves in export markets.

TAFTA and the Difficulties of Institution Building

Chapter 4 shows how cooperation between the central banks in the European Monetary System has taken many years to evolve; even today, that cooperation is fragile. Perhaps, then, a formal system of transatlantic collaboration might be equally shaky, especially in view of the participants' different approaches to the provision of collective business goods. A central concern about a possible TAFTA is that Anglo-Saxon conceptions of market liberalization might be pushed so far as to endanger the provision of collective business goods in Northern Europe; whether heavy costs will be involved in transatlantic cooperation hinges on how difficult it will be to develop institutionalized cooperation. Game theory, as developed over the past two decades, provides some insight into this question, although it also falls short in some respects.

On one hand, game theory has greatly elucidated behavior within institutions—which economists had previously thought of as irrational—

20. Casper (1996); Herrigel (1993); Lutz (1993).
21. Audretsch (1989); Herrigel (1993).

by relating it to equilibrium strategies.[22] Two theoretical developments, the Folk theorem and the concept of perfection, were in large part responsible for this trend in thought. On the other hand, game theory can show how many hypothetical institutional situations embody "rational behavior" without adequately explaining why effective institutions emerge in some real-world situations but not in others.

The Folk theorem may explain how systems for producing collective business goods (such as vocational training) operate, but—it will be argued below—if the systems are at all complex, the theorem's assumptions are satisfied only if prior institutional arrangements exist. It is this condition that determines whether effective institutions will emerge. Hence the fact that Germany's complex systems require strong institutional preconditions may explain why they are difficult to reproduce. The difficulties of developing or reproducing complex systems can be demonstrated by the German vocational training system.[23]

The Folk Theorem and Institutions

The Folk theorem states that, if each member of a group can gain by undertaking some activity as long as a large enough number of the others do, then—even if a dominant strategy called for each participant to opt out—there is some set of credible threats that will ensure that all members will continue their participation, as long as they do not discount future gains too heavily and as long as they believe there is a high enough probability that the activity will continue. The German vocational training system appears to meet these conditions: it depends on widespread participation by companies, individual companies have an incentive to opt out, and there is a high probability in any period that the system will carry on. According to the Folk theorem, the system should then be easy to transfer to other economies (assuming sufficiently low discount rates). Yet attempts to transfer the system have met with only limited success, even in the case of the former German Democratic Republic.[24]

---

22. A notable example was Kreps's (1993) explanation of the rationality of conformity to corporate culture.

23. For discussion of that system, see OECD (1994); Soskice (1994); Streeck and others (1987).

24. Culpepper (1996).

Why is this so? Another condition of the theorem is that the potential participants must have *common knowledge* of three categories of information. Such common knowledge cannot be generated in a short period of time but plausibly requires a whole history of previous cooperation.

The first category of information is the set of strategies that the participants will pursue. They must agree both on the nature of the equilibrium path (in vocational training, this would be the type of training the participants will undertake, the balance between company-specific and marketable skills, the marketability of the skills over the short term or long term, and specific questions about the curricula) and on the nature of the off-the-equilibrium path (that is, what constitutes a deviation, such as neglecting to train or providing inadequate training or putting too much emphasis on company-specific skills). They must also agree on how a company should punish other companies that deviate (for instance, they could withhold orders or let it be known that the company is unreliable), how long the punishment should last, and so on. Clearly, decisionmaking of this complexity requires institutionalized procedures. Moreover, since companies have to make substantial investments in equipment and personnel when setting up their training programs, and since these investments are put at risk if other companies do not adopt similar programs, they have to be confident that institutional procedures will produce common knowledge of the strategies to be adopted.

An analogy can be drawn with a much simpler coordination game, concerning which side of the road to drive on. It brings home the need for confidence that strategies are common knowledge and that all relevant actors look to the same institution for "instruction." In fact people are normally so sure that appropriate strategies are common knowledge in a given country that they take what would otherwise be horrendous risks. It is common knowledge that the government and only the government can decide which side of the road people are to drive on. When the Swedish government changed the side, it was common knowledge to virtually all Swedish drivers. The analogy shows how foolish it would be if policymakers relied on individual drivers to sort out the driving side and how few people would drive if there was no agreement about who set the rules of the road.

The problem is that there is seldom a unique Pareto optimal solution to games of this sort. Although in many cases of Pareto equilibrium all participants are better off, in some instances certain participants will benefit more than others, and vice versa; the structure of the game is comparable to that of the battle of the sexes, as can be seen in a vocational training system. Organize the training curriculum in one way, and small companies with more limited skill requirements will benefit; organize it in another way, and large advanced companies will benefit. The small firms will want lower minimum standards and greater attention to current skills; the large firms will opt for higher standards and more attention to the future capacity to acquire skills. Even within the subbranch of an industry, the training capacities and skill requirements of different companies imply different preferences for Pareto optimal training systems. Even sharper are the differences between the preferences of employers and employees, of current employees and trainees, and of more skilled workers and less skilled workers. Given the great number of agents involved and the need to persuade them that their interests have been properly taken into account, there must be a system of representation and negotiation in which they have confidence.

What circumstances would give rise to such a "high-trust" system at the same time as a vocational training system? Rational actors are prepared to delegate their interests to others when they can see that the "delegates" have good reason to further those interests. In a market economy without well-established representative institutions but with an effective legal system, confidence will arise when it is possible to write contracts that specify at least in broad terms what is expected of delegates. Alternatively, transparent voting and monitoring procedures may be devised, with ultimate recourse to legal action (again a contractual procedure). Where professional reputation, social considerations, or economic pressures are strong enough, individuals may believe that they will be able to threaten delegates credibly with nonlegal sanctions. However, these types of delegation arrangements apply to simple issues where the discretion of the delegate is limited and malperformance can easily be established. Where the issue is complex, the delegate is required to use substantial discretion, and legal recourse is difficult because malperformance cannot easily be established; the rational actor must have the capacity to sanction the delegate individually.

In simple cases collective action may be dealt with in the shadow of the law, without the need for prior institutions; in complex cases it cannot. If participants are to have confidence in an effective system of representation and negotiation affecting a complex issue such as vocational training, two conditions must prevail:

— The system has already established a reputation for effective representation and negotiation among individual companies. This takes time because companies will only have confidence in it if they have seen how it works, or if they can accept the word of other companies that it works effectively.

— Companies also need to believe that they have some means of addressing problems. Since an individual company may have little power, its ties with other companies must be strong enough to ensure that no collective action problem is bringing about a correction.

To reiterate, an effective system of representation and negotiation cannot emerge unless the institutions involved have built up a reputation and underlying companies have close relations with one another.

Under the Folk theorem, a vocational training system also depends on knowledge of "technology," and hence on shared expertise. This shared expertise has to cover a wide spectrum of interrelated subjects: the cost to companies of different training modules, the ability of trainers to implement curricula, the relation of the skills acquired to different patterns of work organization and equipment; the relation between the general education achievements of trainees in different school environments and the general education requirements of different vocational training curricula, the future viability of skills, and so on. When political scientists talk of "epistemic" or "expert" communities, they are assuming that the relevant actors within a vocational training system have common knowledge of the technology of the system. In the terminology of game theory, this corresponds to common knowledge of how to map strategies into payoffs. In the simple examples that are often used to illustrate the Folk theorem, this requirement that common knowledge exists appears easy to satisfy. But in practice its satisfaction depends on a long process of institutional development. In the area of vocational training, the necessary institutions include reasonably formalized ways of resolving disagreements, a means of disseminating information about new developments, and methods of training new experts.

To complicate matters, the building up of expertise depends on flows of information between companies and expert bodies, as well as among companies. The deeper the vocational training, the more important these flows. But herein lies a potential danger for companies: they need to be sure that information about their future technological intentions—which is required to work out the direction in which skills will have to develop—will not be misused. As before, the bodies overseeing vocational training must have a reputation for not misusing information, and companies need to feel confident that cross-company flows of information will not be exploited. To secure such a guarantee, they must have ways of sanctioning other companies.

The third condition that must be met to make the system work, especially in cases where companies do not agree to be sanctioned, is that companies must have common knowledge of one another's activities (this requirement can be weakened somewhat but not in ways relevant to this discussion).[25] In practice this means that the behavior of companies will have to be monitored to some extent. Such monitoring reinforces confidence in the system.

Thus far in the discussion it has been assumed that an effective vocational training system (and a system of technology transfer) could be sustained in equilibrium by appealing to the Folk theorem *if* its conditions concerning common knowledge are met. But a long and strong tradition of institutional development—which is the product of decades of vocational training, to judge by the experience of Switzerland, Austria, and Germany, and by close connections between companies—is necessary for common knowledge assumptions to hold.

Complementarities and Interlocking Systems

It is difficult to build a complex institutional system, such as Germany's vocational training system, for yet another reason: other parts of the institutional framework must also work in particular ways. A vocational training system, for example, depends on some degree of long-term attachment between skilled employees and the company that trains them. This gives both the company and the

25. Fudenberg and Maskin (1986).

trainee an incentive to invest in training in a mixture of marketable and company-specific skills. If such an attachment is to be feasible for the company and credible for the employee, the financial system has to ensure that the company will enjoy a long-term relationship with its owners and lenders, while the industrial relations system has to convince employees—in the German case, through codetermination—that the company is sticking to employment security. But the company must also be reassured that other companies will not be able to poach its skilled workers. Companies will therefore need to cooperate in the development of new skills. This, in turn, implies that the rules of competition permit such cooperation; such cooperation would not be consistent with head-on competition in product markets.

Examples of these kinds of linkages abound in the German institutional framework. They show that an effective vocational training system cannot emerge unless a complex institutional framework is in existence. A related argument can be made about each element of the framework, stated in the language of complementarities: the effectiveness of each of the four components of the German institutional framework discussed in this chapter—the vocational training system, the financial system, the industrial relations systems, and the system governing relations between companies—depends on the effectiveness of the other three.

Two conclusions can be drawn from the foregoing argument. First, in a deregulated framework, any attempt to develop one system in isolation, such as vocational training, would likely fail, since the other systems would have to be operating appropriately before the training system could unfold. Thus, even if the question of the institutional preconditions discussed in the context of the Folk theorem did not arise, the different systems would have to be set up in a coordinated way. How such coordination would take place in deregulated markets is unclear. Second, the institutional preconditions apply in any case to each of the systems. In practical terms, then, it is difficult to see a German-type framework being developed out of a deregulated framework. If a TAFTA entailed a drive toward market liberalization of the Anglo-Saxon variety, and if a German-type institutional framework was vulnerable to this drive, there would be little possibility of recreating a German-type framework at a later date.

Sources of German-Type Vulnerability

German institutions are potentially vulnerable to legal attack in the context of Anglo-Saxon market liberalization for several reasons. To begin with, the modern German economy is already liberal and open in important respects. Since World War II Germany has been one of the strongest proponents of open world markets and minimal restrictions on both inward and outward foreign direct investment (FDI). German companies do not see themselves heavily constrained by their domestic institutional environment (as opposed to high social security costs and an overvalued currency). And since the mid-1980s utilities have been substantially liberalized. The situation is comparable in Sweden and Switzerland.

Thus far there is little evidence to suggest that the German framework would collapse as a result of further liberalization of FDI and imports. Not only has Germany been a liberal player in world markets for some time, but several laws buttress its institutional framework. Following are some notable examples of this legislation:

— Works councils representing employees within companies have been granted the power to codetermine redundancies and overtime and to play a major role in work organization and vocational training.[26]

— Under the collective bargaining system, members of employer associations must comply with regulations governing basic rates of pay and conditions in the workplace, and the government can extend these regulations to all employers in an industry.[27]

— A number of regulations apply to the operation of the vocational training system.[28]

— Rules have been established that make it relatively easy to block hostile takeovers.[29]

It might be argued that many German companies need such laws to safeguard their product-market strategies. If legal supports were withdrawn, they would carry on as before, substituting their own sanctions for legal ones. Some companies would choose not to be members of such "clubs," but that would not damage the overall system as long as enough companies remained club members. This

26. Berghahn and Detlev (1987).
27. Berghahn and Detlev (1987).
28. Streeck (1987).
29. Franks and Mayer (1990).

view is consistent with both Swedish and Japanese experience, where legal constraints do not appear to support the institutional framework to the same extent as in Germany.

The German institutional framework might be vulnerable, however, to much stricter competition rules than at present, particularly in three areas. First, most employment contracts prevent middle and senior managers, if they choose to leave a company, from working in the same area for a period of two years. This means that managers cannot start competitive businesses and that other companies cannot move into a market by hiring managers from their competitors. Such clauses prohibiting competition (*Wettbewerbsverbot*) appear to have been accepted by the courts. Second, stable shareholder agreements, although informal, could be made illegal; in that case public companies would not be able to rely on informal agreements among major shareholders to prevent hostile takeovers. Third, competition policy could use a narrower definition of industries to impose maximum market share requirements and could define those industries on a domestic basis. Moreover, it could eliminate legal cartels and could restrict cooperation between companies.[30]

The German institutional framework would be vulnerable in such cases because companies operating in highly competitive export markets are accustomed to direct and indirect cooperation with other German companies. Cooperative industrial relations; effective vocational training; the system linking universities, research institutes, and companies in the transfer of technology; and long-term finance— all depend on a fairly high degree of trust between companies. That trust, in turn, depends on the extent to which head-on competition between German companies can be avoided.

The Costs and Benefits of TAFTA

The costs and benefits of a TAFTA can be attributed to four factors. First, some benefits of international trade derive from an economy's comparative institutional advantage. As explained earlier, companies functioning in an Anglo-Saxon framework are best suited to solving organizational problems that permit certain patterns of innovation; those located in the Germanic framework can solve organizational

30. Audretsch (1989); Owen Smith (1994).

problems that permit other kinds of innovation. The benefits of trade between the two institutional systems stem, at least in part, from these different patterns of innovation.

Second, these benefits are realized in large part from the existing trading system in which the United States, Canada, the United Kingdom, Germany, and the other member states of the European Union are embedded. Moreover, means exist (the WTO and ad hoc agreements) to negotiate further liberalizing agreements as the parties concerned see fit. It can, of course, be argued that progress would be more rapid in the overarching framework of negotiation that a TAFTA would provide. For example, governments might find it easier to organize compensatory side payments to losers when there are simultaneous winners within the national jurisdiction; winners may also give a government the political and electoral resources to face down concurrent losers. But the significant point is that no self-evidently massive gains can be expected from trade through a TAFTA that could not otherwise be brought about. This underlines the initial observation that the impetus behind a TAFTA is political rather than economic.

Third, it has been said that entering into a TAFTA would erase the institutional differences between the Northern European and the Anglo-Saxon economies. But why should this be so when the far-reaching integration of national economies already accomplished in Europe has not so far had that effect? To begin with, the development of European economic integration over the past four decades was accompanied by a push toward a common system of industrial relations and corporate governance. Collective bargaining was widely accepted, and from the mid-1960s there was a prolonged attempt to realize a European Works Council Directive (EWCD). As it happens, this directive has recently been promulgated, but in a watered-down form. The EWCD was anathema to the U.K. conservative governments of the 1980s and 1990s. For their part, U.K. governments have so far prevented a European company law directive; again, the original idea was to develop a directive along the lines of German company law, and thus to include both dual boards and employee representation on the supervisory board. If, as now seems possible, an EWCD sees the light of day, it will most likely be voluntary and will impose on a company that uses it neither dual boards nor board-level employee representation (the advantage of EWCD will simply be that separate incorporation in different member states will not be required). The minimalist nature of these directives reflects strong battles between different institutional frameworks, with the result that individual countries have reached a stand-off: they can keep their own institutions. Apparently Margaret Thatcher believed that the Single European Act would bring about an American-style Europe of highly competitive markets. But other European countries did not want this and fenced off whole areas from the discussions: thus collective bargaining, vocational training, takeover rules, technology transfer, and intercompany cooperation rules did not enter into the list of areas to be liberalized. Although companies are allowed to go to the European Court of Justice to argue for measures of liberalization in cases that contravene the Treaty of Rome, the European Commission has been cautious in its interpretations. As a consequence, the development of the European Union has allowed neither an Anglo-Saxon deregulated model nor a continental model to take over (or be imposed on the United Kingdom).

Furthermore, a TAFTA is more likely than the Single European Act to impose a deregulated Anglo-Saxon market model on the member states of the European Union. It is easier to break down institutional collaboration of the kind prevalent in Germany than to build it up. Development usually takes place over long periods of time and requires the building up of trust, of shared expertise and understanding, of agreed and understood procedures for changing rules in reaction to external shocks, and of agreed and effective methods of sanctioning those who do not cooperate. Dismantling, by contrast, needs a legal prohibition on certain types of contact and agreement between companies.

From this perspective, the problem with TAFTA lies in the areas that will be subject to liberalization and in the procedures that will be set up to permit legal and political challenges to practices in different countries. Will competition policy, the market for corporate governance (the conduct of takeovers, interests of nonshareholder "stakeholders" such as employees), the market for research and development, and labor markets (including vocational training, wage determination, and employee codetermination rights) be considered areas of legitimate concern of a TAFTA? And, if they are, what recourse will governments and private actors have to legal, political, or arbitral action in the event of breaches of TAFTA? Neither of these questions can be answered before a TAFTA is agreed. Once procedures for adjudicating a breach have been established, they may easily take on a life of their own.

The danger from the United States, first and foremost, is that it would be a far stronger player in negotiating a TAFTA than was the United Kingdom in bargaining over the Single European Act. But U.S. interests—the extension of a deregulated environment de jure and de facto for American companies abroad—are similar. Furthermore, the possibility that the U.S. government might use its political power—or that large American companies might develop adversarial legal strategies to pursue a deregulatory agenda—depends on the nature of TAFTA and its procedures for resolving disputes. But procedures for breach might be established that would lend themselves to these scenarios. Arrangements in economies such as that of Germany might then be vulnerable to challenge.

The preceding arguments should in no way be construed as casting doubt on the central importance of free trade across the North Atlantic (or more widely). The question being raised here is simply whether the deepening of economic relations implied by a TAFTA would destroy or weaken the complex institutions in Germany (and other economies in continental Europe) that may well confer on it comparative institutional advantage and enable German-located companies to produce goods that are difficult to produce in North America or the United Kingdom. The much more deregulated environment in North America and the United Kingdom in turn provides comparative institutional advantage in another range of goods and services. The cause for concern in the TAFTA debate is that, at the moment, the emphasis is on political considerations that give little attention to questions of comparative institutional advantage in international trade.

How serious are the problems raised in this chapter? Some might argue that the German system is like a dinosaur collapsing under its own weight and that such questions are therefore irrelevant. This position clearly misinterprets the current situation.[31] Even more questionable is the description of possible American strategy in the shaping and use of a TAFTA. If the U.S. government were a rational actor and were concerned about maximizing the welfare of the

31. Carlin and Soskice (1997).

median voter, the description here would be completely off the mark. If it accepted the logic of this chapter, the U.S. government would not want to impose an Anglo-Saxon institutional framework on Germany since that would reduce the benefit of comparative institutional advantage.

The problem with this hypothesis lies in the mainsprings of government behavior; in particular, the operation of Congress allows particular interest groups to pressure the administration in the conduct of its commercial policy. A recent report on U.S.-Japanese negotiations over access to the Japanese insurance market might well be a fitting conclusion to this chapter, even though its subject is not Germany: "A resolution to the dispute depends on significant deregulation of the private sector. But the Japanese authorities and industry protest that Japan is being asked to give up a system with which they are extremely comfortable and adopt one that is alien to Japanese culture." The Japanese are particularly worried about the disruptive effects that a sudden injection of competition would have on a society that treasures harmony and on a tried and tested system in which regulation may have kept choice limited and prices high but has ensured that insurance is widely and equally available.[32]

32. *Financial Times*, June 12, 1996.

Chapter 3

Whither U.S.-EU Trade Relations?

Jeffrey J. Schott

The United States and the European Union are the two ele-
phants of the world trading system. Together they
account for 55 percent of global output and about 40 percent of world
exports (excluding intra-EU trade). Their actions, whether in concert
or opposition, have significant implications for their neighbors and
trading partners, so it is not surprising that the bilateral relationship
commands attention.

On the whole, bilateral relations between the United States and
Europe have been good throughout the post–World War II period.
Close trade relations were part of the global strategy to revitalize
Europe so it could better meet and deter the threat from the Soviet
Union, and bilateral trade disputes were defused by and large in def-
erence to broader strategic interests of the Western alliance.[1] Despite
frictions over agriculture and industrial subsidies, bilateral disputes
were managed cordially and rarely exhibited the political rancor so
common to U.S.-Japan, and more recently U.S.-China, trade relations.

Cooperation and conflict have also been the hallmark of trade relations between the United States and Europe in the General Agreement on Tariffs and Trade (GATT) and in its successor body, the
World Trade Organization (WTO). Both regions play an important
leadership role in the world trading system and have used the
GATT/WTO forum to negotiate solutions to bilateral problems, or to

The author would like to thank Franscesc Balcells-Forellad, Gena Morgan, and
Shanna Rose for their assistance in compiling the tables for this chapter.
1. Patterson (1966) describes how such considerations prompted GATT members
to accept European integration arrangements despite concerns about their consistency
with international trade rules.

bring legal challenges against practices of the other side.[2] Their combined market power affords them substantial influence in setting the agenda for multilateral trade negotiations, and in crafting agreements that often codify their own domestic practices in international trading rules.

Over the past three decades, both regions have increasingly turned to multilateral trade negotiations to mitigate bilateral trade problems. The Kennedy Round (1963–67) reduced tensions stemming from European integration and the European Community's common agricultural policy (CAP). The Tokyo Round (1973–79) developed new rules on subsidies and antidumping, government procurement, and other nontariff barriers that resolved among other things the long-standing bilateral dispute over the American selling-price system of customs valuation. Most recently, the Uruguay Round (1986–94) achieved grudging but nonetheless important reforms covering agricultural subsidies and import barriers (even though U.S.-EU bilateral disputes over these issues significantly impeded the GATT talks and almost caused their collapse).

Since the conclusion of the Uruguay Round, however, new questions have arisen about the health of the bilateral trade relationship, prompted primarily by two related concerns:

— The first concern is that the U.S.-EU relationship has been relegated to the back burner as both sides pursue their respective regional initiatives (the United States in the Asia-Pacific region and Western Hemisphere, the European Union in Central and Eastern Europe and the Mediterranean Basin).

— The second concern is that different security priorities in the post–cold war era are provoking new trade frictions between the erstwhile allies in the Persian Gulf and other regions.

In response, government officials have sought to kill two birds with one stone by proposing (in various forms) a new transatlantic trade initiative that would redress the problem of "attention diversion" and seek to cement the transatlantic alliance through new economic treaty obligations. Curiously, the new proposals have em-

2. The United States has been the undisputed leader of the GATT system and demandeur for all eight rounds of multilateral negotiations in the postwar period; the European Union has been the other main protagonist and now occasionally assumes the leadership mantle on sectoral issues (such as those relating to financial services and investment).

anated primarily from foreign policy officials rather than economic officials and seem to downplay both the areas of existing cooperation and the long-standing problems that limit the scope for new bilateral treaty arrangements. Before postulating a cure for the perceived ills of the transatlantic trade relationship, however, it would seem sensible to first examine the patient. To that end, this chapter reviews recent U.S.-EU trade and investment flows, analyzes existing ånd potential problem areas, and recommends how the two regions can work together over the near to medium term to strengthen their bilateral trade relations.

U.S.-EU Trade and Investment: 1990–96

The United States and the European Union maintain the world's second largest trade partnership, with the volume of bilateral merchandise trade (which reached $270 billion in 1996) almost equal to that of the United States and Canada ($290 billion). Between 1990 and 1996 the EU shares of total U.S. merchandise exports and imports averaged 22 percent and 18 percent, respectively (table 3-1).[3] However, the growth of bilateral trade (42 percent) has been much slower than growth of total U.S. trade (60 percent), and the EU share of total U.S. trade has consequently declined somewhat during this period.

Over the same period, total U.S. trade with the Four Tigers of East Asia (Singapore, Hong Kong, Taiwan, and South Korea) plus China grew by 83 percent, and U.S. trade with Mexico by 124 percent, lending credence to the view that U.S. trading interests are being refocused on other regions. By contrast, the U.S. bilateral trade balance with the European Union during this period has been relatively small compared to the overall volume of trade, and thus has not provoked the sharp political reaction in Congress that marks U.S. relations with China, Japan, and Mexico in the aftermath of the North American Free Trade Agreement.

Almost half of all U.S. merchandise exports to the European Union during 1990–96 consisted of machinery and transport equipment, which falls under category 7 of the SITC (table 3-2). Another quarter is covered by shipments of chemicals (SITC 5) and miscellaneous manu-

---

3. The United States does not command quite as large a share of EU trade. In 1995 trade with the United States accounted for 17 percent of total EU trade (excluding intra-EU flows).

TABLE 3-1. *U.S. Trade with the European Union, 1985–96*[a]

Millions of U.S. dollars unless otherwise indicated

Year	Exports	EU share of U.S. exports (percent)	Imports	EU share of U.S. imports (percent)	Trade balance
1985	48,264	22.0	67,822	19.6	–19,588
1986	52,377	23.0	75,736	20.5	–23,360
1987	59,732	23.6	81,188	20.0	–21,456
1988	74,769	23.2	84,942	19.2	–10,262
1989	86,952	23.8	85,129	18.0	1,463
1990	98,024	24.9	91,868	18.5	6,156
1991	103,208	24.5	86,841	17.7	16,727
1992	102,845	23.0	94,050	17.7	8,795
1993	96,957	20.9	98,007	16.9	–1,051
1994	107,750	21.0	119,457	18.0	–11,707
1995	123,599	21.2	131,910	17.7	–8,311
1996	127,511	20.4	142,718	18.0	–15,208

Source: U.S. Department of Commerce.

a. Data for 1985–93 cover EU-12; data for 1994–96 cover EU-15.

factured products (SITC 8). Agricultural products (SITC 0, 1, and 4) accounted for 6 percent of total U.S. exports. Since 1990 U.S. exports have expanded most sharply in the areas of animal and vegetable oils (up 62 percent) and chemicals (up 39 percent). The profile of U.S. imports from the European Union is similar, except that EU shipments of manufactured goods under SITC 6 are more than double U.S. exports and have grown by about 34 percent during this period.

U.S. trade with Western Europe in private services is also robust.[4] In 1996 U.S. private service exports to Western Europe totaled $76.3 billion and imports reached $53.1 billion, representing 34 percent and 37 percent of total U.S. private services trade, respectively. Over the period 1990–96, U.S. private services exports and imports to and from Western Europe grew by 58 percent and 35 percent, respectively.[5]

4. Because of the change in EU membership, I have substituted data from Western Europe on services trade, and the figures are slightly larger than the trade of the EU-15 countries.

5. All data are from the Bureau of Economic Analysis, *Survey of Current Business,* various years. Data have been adjusted to exclude government services.

TABLE 3-2. *U.S.-EU Trade, by Commodity, 1990–96*[a]

Millions of U.S. dollars

SITC rev 3 commodity	1990	1991	1992	1993	1994	1995	1996
Total U.S. exports (f.a.s. value) to European Union							
0. Food and live animals	3,949	4,171	4,179	4,003	4,130	4,744	4,800
1. Beverages and tobacco	2,765	2,313	2,225	1,881	2,717	2,790	2,590
2. Crude materials, inedible, except fuels	6,589	6,054	6,381	5,393	5,804	7,865	7,126
3. Mineral fuels, lubricants, related materials	3,844	4,100	3,228	2,240	1,955	2,523	2,706
4. Animal and vegetable oils, fats, and waxes	163	195	275	197	248	291	264
5. Chemicals and related products	11,045	11,752	12,540	11,737	13,056	15,095	15,333
6. Manufactures classified chiefly by material	6,360	6,721	6,577	6,064	6,642	8,770	8,808
7. Machinery and transport equipment	51,219	54,598	52,460	48,286	53,376	60,409	62,637
8. Miscellaneous manufactured items	13,252	14,272	15,056	14,099	13,918	15,523	16,154
9. Commodity and transaction not classified elsewhere	4,303	4,326	4,813	7,582	5,902	5,591	7,094
10. Total	103,489	108,502	107,733	101,483	107,750	123,599	127,511
Total U.S. imports (customs value) from European Union							
0. Food and live animals	2,282	2,327	2,290	2,254	2,576	2,702	2,871
1. Beverages and tobacco	2,929	2,753	3,132	2,929	3,133	3,284	3,759
2. Crude materials, inedible, except fuels	1,140	1,063	1,087	1,196	1,246	1,366	1,351
3. Mineral fuels, lubricants, and related materials	4,623	3,119	3,542	3,826	5,012	3,824	4,284
4. Animal and vegetable oils, fats, and waxes	294	306	322	286	289	354	461
5. Chemicals and related products	10,129	10,890	12,559	12,819	13,936	16,493	19,398
6. Manufactures classified chiefly by material	15,008	13,738	14,010	15,573	18,275	19,070	20,072
7. Machinery and transport equipment	43,335	40,851	44,715	46,297	52,393	59,504	62,713
8. Miscellaneous manufactured items	14,885	13,730	14,432	15,092	16,848	19,058	20,607
9. Commodity and transaction not classified elsewhere	4,841	4,568	5,170	5,285	5,750	6,256	7,203
10. Total	99,466	93,346	101,258	105,559	119,457	131,910	142,718

Source: U.S. Department of Commerce.

a. Data for 1990–96 cover EU-15. All figures, including totals, have been rounded off from thousands of U.S. dollars.

U.S. exports of commercial services between unaffiliated firms almost doubled during the period 1990–95, and totaled about $13 billion in 1995 (18 percent of total U.S. service exports to Europe). Leading the export surge were business services (where U.S. receipts almost tripled), particularly sales of computers, data processing, and legal services.

In brief, the U.S.-EU trade flows are large and relatively balanced. Merchandise trade has expanded more rapidly than output in both regions but less rapidly than U.S. trade with other regions. Farm products account for a small share of bilateral trade, although the volume of trade here is clearly constrained by trade barriers and domestic subsidies on both sides of the ocean. Bilateral trade in services has been booming.

Given these trends, what evidence exists that bilateral trade has been significantly hampered by tariff and nontariff trade barriers? The answer is not much. Results from both computable general equilibrium (CGE) and gravity models indicate that little additional trade could be expected in the absence of bilateral industrial tariffs.[6] One such CGE analysis reports that bilateral tariff reform, coupled with the full liberalization of farm trade barriers and the removal of antidumping duties, would yield more substantial results in both regions (a gain of 0.2 to 0.4 percent of GDP, and an increase of 5 to 6 percent in exports).[7] Not surprisingly, it concludes that U.S. and EU gains from global liberalization would swamp the benefits of bilateral initiatives.

What distinguishes the U.S.-EU relationship from others is not the volume of trade but rather the direct investment of each party in the other's market. At the end of 1995, the total stock of two-way direct investment reached $640 billion. Tables 3-3 and 3-4 tell the story.

In 1995 U.S. foreign direct investment (FDI) in the European Union reached $315 billion on a historical cost basis and accounted for 44 percent of total U.S. overseas direct investment. By comparison, Canada, the largest U.S. trading partner, hosted 11.4 percent of total U.S. FDI, and Japan had just 5.5 percent. More than half of U.S. FDI in the EU-15 is in services, primarily financial services ($116 billion, or 37 percent of total U.S. FDI in the European Union). Manufacturing accounts for almost 40 percent of U.S. FDI, chemicals being in the lead

6. See Baldwin and Francois (1996); Frankel (1997).
7. Baldwin and Francois (1996).

TABLE 3-3. *U.S. Foreign Direct Investment in the EU-15 (Historical-Cost Basis), 1990–95*[a]

Millions of U.S. dollars unless otherwise indicated

Investment	1990	1991	1992	1993	1994	1995	Global U.S. FDI (1995) Value	EU-15 share (percent)
Total	180,682	192,059	213,760	239,581	256,081	315,378	711,621	44.3
Manufacturing	81,871 (45.3)	87,153 (45.4)	90,435 (42.3)	91,377 (38.1)	103,340 (40.4)	124,232 (39.4)	257,589	48.2
Chemicals	17,949 (9.9)	18,906 (9.8)	24,848 (11.6)	25,530 (10.7)	28,594 (11.2)	42,777 (13.6)	68,082	62.8
Petroleum	17,748 (9.8)	17,810 (9.3)	20,844 (9.8)	21,404 (8.9)	21,012 (8.2)	21,280 (6.7)	69,653	30.6
Services	76,511 (42.3)	80,870 (42.1)	97,306 (45.5)	120,998 (50.5)	125,448 (49.0)	159,548 (50.6)	341,710	46.7
Financial services[b]	56,140 (31.1)	56,729 (29.5)	66,535 (31.1)	88,576 (37.0)	87,579 (34.2)	115,929 (36.8)	242,530	47.8
Wholesale trade	14,382 (8.0)	17,469 (9.1)	20,466 (9.6)	20,711 (8.6)	24,581 (9.6)	26,648 (8.4)	71,354	37.3
Other industries	4,096 (2.3)	5,040 (2.6)	6,016 (2.8)	6,078 (2.5)	6,544 (2.6)	10,317 (3.3)	42,668	24.2
Total U.S. FDI abroad	424,086	450,196	502,063	559,733	612,109	711,621		
EU-15 share (percent)	42.6	42.7	42.6	42.8	41.8	44.3		
Canada share (percent)	15.8	15.2	13.7	12.4	11.9	11.4		
Japan share (percent)	4.9	5.0	5.3	5.6	6.0	5.5		

Source: U.S. Department of Commerce, Survey of Current Business, various issues.
a. Figures in parentheses are percentages.
b. Including real estate.

TABLE 3-4. *EU-15 Foreign Direct Investment in the United States, 1990–95 (Historical-Cost Basis)s 1990–95[a]*

Millions of U.S. dollars unless otherwise indicated

Investment	1990	1991	1992	1993	1994	1995	Total FDI in U.S. (1995) Value	Total FDI in U.S. (1995) EU share (percent)
Total	232,050	236,415	235,202	263,451	285,403	325,364	560,088	58.1
Manufacturing	110,446 (47.6)	103,575 (43.8)	104,469 (44.4)	112,664 (42.8)	123,174 (43.2)	142,235 (43.7)	210,312	67.6
Chemicals	36,335 (15.7)	40,412 (17.1)	41,232 (17.5)	48,181 (18.3)	52,901 (18.5)	59,722 (18.4)	76,523	78.0
Petroleum	33,420 (14.4)	31,371 (13.3)	29,083 (12.4)	23,996 (9.1)	25,349 (8.9)	26,183 (8.0)	35,636	73.5
Services	67,957 (29.3)	78,232 (33.1)	79,448 (33.8)	99,085 (37.6)	104,466 (36.6)	124,777 (38.3)	260,083	48.0
Financial services	25,214 (10.9)	31,992 (13.5)	36,485 (15.5)	56,476 (21.4)	55,449 (19.4)	72,776 (22.4)	137,067	53.1
Wholesale and retail trade	25,812 (11.1)	27,839 (11.8)	25,295 (10.8)	26,554 (10.1)	31,547 (11.1)	33,869 (10.4)	85,086	39.8
Other industries[b]	27,635 (11.9)	23,106 (9.8)	23,809 (10.1)	27,902 (10.6)	33,446 (11.7)	32,170 (9.9)	54,057	59.5
Total FDI in U.S.	396,702	419,108	427,566	464,110	504,401	560,088		
EU-15 share (percent)	58.5	56.4	55.0	56.8	56.6	58.1		
Japan share (percent)	20.6	22.7	23.3	21.4	20.4	19.4		
Canada share (percent)	7.6	8.8	8.9	8.6	8.6	8.2		

Source: U.S. Department of Commerce, *Survey of Current Business,* various issues.
a. Figures in parentheses are percentages.
b. Including real estate.

with $43 billion invested. Investment in the petroleum sector has remained flat; as a share of total U.S. FDI, it declined to 7 percent. Over the period 1990–95, U.S. FDI in the EU-15 grew by 75 percent, whereas global U.S. FDI increased 68 percent.

In contrast, EU-15 direct investments in the United States over the same period grew by 40 percent and totaled $325 billion at the end of 1995, which represents 58 percent of all FDI in the United States. Japan and Canada account for 19 percent and 8 percent, respectively. EU companies have invested somewhat more in manufacturing ($142 billion) than in services ($125 billion) but, as with U.S. investments in the EU-15, chemicals ($60 billion) and financial services ($73 billion) are the favored sectors. EU firms account for 78 percent and 53 percent of all foreign investors in the United States in those respective sectors.

The fact that each region has an important ownership stake in the other's market has exerted a strong positive impact on bilateral trade relations. Imports by U.S. affiliates from their EU parent firms and exports by U.S. parents to their EU affiliates account for roughly one-third of total U.S. imports from and exports to the European Union. These firms have a vested interest in maintaining cordial bilateral relations and generally oppose the imposition of new trade restrictions. Perhaps more important, bilateral FDI concentrates on sectors in which both regions are globally competitive, such as financial and professional services and chemicals. FDI in these sectors serves both the regional market and exports and has created domestic constituencies supportive of multilateral trade liberalization, as is clear from their leadership in sectoral initiatives in the Uruguay Round and in the WTO.

Sources of Bilateral Trade Friction

Given the volume of bilateral trade flows, it is not surprising that trade officials in both regions face a continuing stream of complaints about the laws, regulations, and trade practices of the other side. The record of recent U.S.-EU trade confrontations yields important information on the major areas of current trade disputes and potential trade friction, which range from small registered complaints about foreign practices to formal disputes brought to the GATT/WTO or initiated under various domestic unfair trade statutes.

Trade Complaints

The United States and the European Union issue annual reports on trade barriers maintained by the other side. The reports describe a laundry list of national practices that industry and government officials in the other region are concerned about and that may or may not generate formal trade disputes. Interestingly, both sets of reports cover similar categories of trade barriers: import policies; standards, testing, labeling, and certification practices; government procurement practices; export subsidies; intellectual property issues; barriers to trade in services and investment; and other miscellaneous practices. Tables 3A-1 and 3A-2 document the number of complaints in each category.

U.S. COMPLAINTS. U.S. complaints center on four main areas: agricultural policies, intellectual property rights, standards and certification requirements, and services and investment policy. Many of these complaints relate to issues that are not yet covered by WTO disciplines or that previous negotiations have not yet fully resolved (for example, discriminatory procurement rules and investment restrictions applied by EU member states). In some of these cases, the complaints reflect unfulfilled U.S. objectives from the Uruguay Round. Other complaints are directed at alleged violations of WTO obligations in matters such as the implementation of farm trade concessions, compensation claims arising from EU enlargement, and food product standards (for example, for hormone-treated meat and genetically altered soybeans).

Still other U.S. complaints draw attention to areas of public policy that impose significant costs on traded goods (such as testing and certification requirements). These may be classified as agenda-setting initiatives since they reflect the desire of the U.S. business community to see governments develop common regulatory practices, notably through the negotiation of mutual recognition agreements (MRAs). Interest in MRAs is high because about 60 percent of U.S. merchandise exports to the European Union in 1993 were subject to product certification requirements.[8]

EU COMPLAINTS. EU complaints about U.S. practices focus more on long-standing U.S. restrictions on trade and investment in specific

8. Wilson (1996, p. 7)

service sectors (financial, maritime, telecommunications, and air transport) and a broad array of U.S. policies arising from trade, tax, and sanctions legislation. In 1996 about 27 percent of EU complaints targeted U.S. laws—such as the Glass-Steagall and Jones acts or telecommunications legislation and regulatory actions (or proposals) by the Federal Communications Commission—that impede access to or activity in the U.S. services market even though they may not contravene U.S. international obligations.

Almost 24 percent of EU complaints pertained to the implementation of U.S. trade laws and statutes that mandate the imposition of economic sanctions for nontrade purposes. Some of these are longstanding complaints about section 301 of U.S. trade law, which is designed to enforce U.S. rights under international trade agreements and combat unfair foreign trade practices, and which has been used to retaliate against EU agricultural, product certification, and telecommunications procurement practices. Others are directed against the Helms-Burton and Iran and Libya Sanctions acts, which threaten the extraterritorial imposition of U.S. sanctions against European firms doing business in Cuba, Iran, and Libya, and at various U.S. tax practices at the federal and state level (such as luxury and gas-guzzler auto taxes and state policies regarding the unitary taxation of corporate income).

To be sure, agriculture and standards/certification are also areas of EU concern, but they do not figure as prominently as in the U.S. reports. About 5 percent of EU complaints in 1996 were about farm policies, most notably U.S. farm export subsidies and dairy quotas, as well as newer policies covering domestic content of tobacco products, the alleged misuse of geographical appellations for wine, sanitary and phytosanitary standards, and drift-net fishing regulations (in the notorious "Tuna-Dolphin" case). And about 10 percent of total EU complaints were directed at federal and state product standards, testing and certification procedures, and labeling requirements; here, the concerns were similar to those raised by U.S. firms.[9] Regulatory practices of the Food and Drug Administration, and U.S. statutes such as the 1990 Fastener Quality Act and the Nutrition Labeling and Education Act also drew some protests.

---

9. Illustrative of such cases is the EU challenge of U.S. CAFE (corporate average fuel economy) standards for automobiles.

Legal Actions

Some of the foregoing complaints eventually develop into formal disputes that are filed with the GATT/WTO or are pursued under domestic unfair trade laws (especially antidumping/countervail and U.S. section 301 cases). These cases set out the priority concerns of each side that can be redressed through remedies sanctioned by the international trade rules. The following subsections summarize the recent bilateral case load arising from GATT/WTO disputes, antidumping, and U.S. section 301 cases.

GATT/WTO DISPUTES. Since 1990 (through 1997) twenty-three bilateral disputes have been brought to the GATT/WTO (see table 3-5). Ten of these cases involve disputed practices or policies affecting farm or processed agricultural products that were unresolved in previous trade negotiations or otherwise allegedly ran afoul of GATT obligations. Other cases span a broad range of practices from harbor fees, auto taxes, customs reclassification of computer equipment, and enforcement of intellectual property rights to the notorious Helms-Burton law providing extraterritorial application of U.S. sanctions against Cuba.

Interestingly, several of the older GATT cases have remained active because disputants were able to block GATT findings and recommendations. New WTO dispute procedures preclude such practices and require almost automatic acceptance of panel or appellate body rulings. As a consequence, many cases are now settled out of court, before panel reports are issued.[10] Several recent EU-U.S. cases were settled early, including the bilateral dispute over the European Union's concession on grains in the Uruguay Round.

ANTIDUMPING/COUNTERVAIL CASES. The United States and the European Union are the leading practitioners of antidumping, so it is not surprising that some actions are directed against the trade of the other. The United States also invokes its countervailing duty (CVD) statute against EU subsidies, although it is doing so with declining frequency. During the period 1990–95, the United States initiated nineteen CVD and seventy-six antidumping cases against the trade of the EU-15 countries; roughly two-thirds of these involved steel prod-

10. See Schott (1996, esp. chaps. 1 and 9).

TABLE 3-5. *GATT/WTO Disputes*

Dispute	Case number	Consultation request date	Disputed practice or policy
GATT (1990–94)			
U.S. v. EEC	: : :	11/8/90	Restrictions on imports of pork and beef
U.S. v. EEC	: : :	9/17/91	Measures affecting imports of corn gluten feed
EEC v. U.S.	: : :	2/21/92	Restrictions on tuna imports (*Tuna-Dolphin* case)
EEC v. U.S.	: : :	3/20/92	Harbor maintenance fees
EEC v. U.S.	: : :	5/20/92	Taxes on imported autos
EEC v. U.S.	: : :	10/6/93	Measures affecting the import and internal sale of tobacco
WTO (1995–97)			
U.S. v. EU	WT/DS 13	7/19/95	Import levies on grains (regarding Uruguay Round concession)
U.S. et al. v. EU	WT/DS 16	9/28/95	Import regime for bananas
U.S. v. EU	WT/DS 26	1/26/96	Ban on imports of hormone-treated meat
U.S. v. Portugal	WT/DS 37	4/30/96	Patent provisions of Industrial Property Act
EU v. U.S.	WT/DS 38	5/3/96	Helms-Burton law (regarding Cuban sanctions)

EU v. U.S.	WT/DS 39	4/17/96	U.S. retaliation in meat hormones case
U.S. v. EU	WT/DS 62[a]	11/8/96	Customs classification of computer equipment
EU v. U.S.	WT/DS 63	11/28/96	Antidumping measures on imports of solid urea
U.S. v. Belgium	WT/DS 80/1	5/2/97	Restrictions on the provision of commercial telephone directory services
U.S. v. Ireland	WT/DS 82/1	5/14/97	IP obligations regarding copyright and negotiating rights
U.S. v. Denmark	WT/DS 83/1	5/14/97	Enforcement of certain IPRs
EU v. U.S.	WT/DS 85/1	5/23/97	U.S. rules of origin for textiles and apparel
U.S. v. Sweden	WT/DS 86/1	5/28/97	Enforcement of certain IPRs
EU v. U.S.	WT/DS 88/1[b]	6/20/97	Government procurement restrictions by the state of Massachusetts against firms doing business with Burma
EU v. U.S.	WT/DS 100/1	8/18/97	Ban on imports of poultry and products
U.S. v. EU	WT/DS 104/1	10/8/97	Subsidies granted on processed cheese
EU v. U.S.	WT/DS 108/1	11/18/97	Special tax treatment for "foreign sales corporations"

Sources: WTO secretariat data: http://www.wto.org/wto/dispute/bulletin.htm.; GATT, "Guide to GATT Law and Practice," 6th ed., Geneva, 1994, analytical index.

a. Request also extended to United Kingdom (WT/DS 67) and Ireland (WT/DS 68) on February 14, 1997.

b. Request also resubmitted as WT/DS 95 on July 18, 1997.

ucts. Almost half of these cases ended in negative final determinations and thus did not result in the imposition of definitive duties.

By contrast, the EU initiated only four antidumping cases against U.S. firms out of a total of 166 cases over the period 1990–94.[11] Interestingly, despite the imbalance in the caseload, the abuse of antidumping actions has not been a source of bilateral friction, except in the steel sector, because both sides rely on this trade measure as a key weapon in their arsenal against unfair trade policies of other countries. Indeed, the United States and the European Union worked closely together in the Uruguay Round to revise WTO antidumping rules so that they could more effectively use their national statutes against dumped exports from third countries.[12]

U.S. SECTION 301 CASES. The Trade Act of 1974 provided new authority in section 301 Trade to promote the enforcement of U.S. rights under international trade agreements. Between 1975 and 1995, the United States initiated 101 cases under section 301, 34 of which were directed against practices of EU-15 members. EU agricultural export subsidies affecting U.S. competition in third markets and other farm trade issues accounted for 23 of the 34, or 68 percent, of the EU cases;[13] 7 cases involved steel subsidies in EU member states. Three cases involved compensation claims arising from the terms of EU enlargement in 1986 and 1995.

Delineating the Bilateral Trade Agenda

The cases just mentioned provide a rough idea of the sources of trade friction that could affect bilateral trade relations over the near term. At the risk of oversimplification, the following summary points out the main areas of contention reported by each region.

The concerns of the United States are centered on three main areas. The first is the EU's common agricultural policy, which is likely to be exacerbated by the prospective extension of EU farm support programs to new members in Central and Eastern Europe. Agricultural issues account for the large majority of bilateral disputes in the

11. See European Commission (1995).

12. See Schott (1994).

13. Overall, agricultural practices accounted for about one-quarter of all U.S. section 301 cases.

GATT/WTO and of cases brought under U.S. section 301. This trend is likely to continue over the near to medium term. Second are product standards and patent protection, especially in high-technology sectors such as pharmaceuticals, telecommunications equipment, computer hardware and software, and biotechnologies. The third area is government support (via subsidies and preferential procurement) for state-owned enterprises (such as Airbus).

For its part, the European Union is less troubled by traditional trade barriers and has shifted its focus to areas in which U.S.-EU trade friction is likely to expand (for example, investment and services, and environmental issues). In addition, EU officials are finding more and more fault with legislative initiatives and actions by subfederal governments; the most important of these concerns the imposition of U.S. economic sanctions. For example, recent U.S. legislation providing for the extraterritorial application of U.S. sanctions against Cuba and Iran has created a furor in Europe and elsewhere and prompted several governments to implement legal countermeasures that would offset the economic impact of prospective U.S. actions on their firms.[14]

All of these issues raise delicate legal and jurisdictional problems. To resolve many of these problems U.S. trade officials will have to coordinate with and sometimes counteract legislative mandates emanating from the federal, state, or local levels.

The EU and U.S. reports focus primarily on access to each other's markets; the main worry in connection with EU-U.S. competition in third-country markets is agricultural export subsidies. Neither side gives much attention to tariff liberalization as a means of improving access to each regional market.

Tariffs seem to be regarded as more of a problem in third-country markets than in transatlantic trade—hence the interest of both sides in pursuing "zero-for-zero" tariff deals in the WTO. To be sure, the average trade-weighted tariff on bilateral trade will be very low after the full implementation of the Uruguay Round liberalization. However, tariff peaks will remain in a number of product sectors, particularly in agriculture, owing to the "dirty" tariffication of non-tariff barriers resulting from the Uruguay Round commitments. After

14. These actions echo the European response to U.S. attempts in the early 1980s to block foreign subsidiaries of U.S. corporations from supplying equipment for the construction of a gas pipeline from the Soviet Union to Western Europe.

full implementation of Uruguay Round liberalization in 2000, EU tariff bindings on dairy (178 percent) and sugar (152 percent) will exceed even the nearly triple-digit levels of U.S. bindings on those products.[15] Tariff peaks also exist in the textile and apparel and electronics sectors, although the latter will be eliminated under the Information Technology Agreement (ITA).

Two other issues are notable, because of their omission from the complaint catalogs issued by the United States and the European Union: the first has to do with "rival" or competitive regionalism and the second with the implications of European Monetary Union (EMU) for transatlantic trade. The former lies directly in the domain of trade officials; the latter requires coherent trade and macroeconomic policies. (For more on these issues, see the next section and also chapter 4.)

REGIONALISM. Over the past decade, the United States and the European Union have repeatedly turned to regional negotiations both to strengthen ties with trading partners near and far and to supplement multilateral trade initiatives through regional "GATT-Plus" accords. The United States has built the North American Free Trade Agreement through a series of negotiations with Canada and Mexico and has sought to expand NAFTA disciplines to Chile and to the twenty-four participating countries in the Caribbean Basin Initiative in order to lay the foundation for the conclusion of negotiations on a hemisphere-wide Free Trade Area of the Americas by 2005. The United States has also joined with seventeen other countries in the Asia-Pacific Economic Cooperation (APEC) forum in committing to the achievement of free trade and investment in the Asia-Pacific region by 2010 for most members and 2020 for developing countries.

The European Union has been equally active, albeit within a narrower geographic zone. Throughout the 1990s the European Union has both deepened its regional integration through the single-market initiatives mandated by the Single European Act of 1985 and continued the process of widening EU membership: Austria, Finland, and Sweden joined the Union in 1995, and new association arrangements have been negotiated with prospective members in Central and Eastern Europe. In addition, the European Union has extended free-trade commitments (at least in industrial products with a few excep-

15. See Schott (1996, p. 18).

tions) to its neighbors in the Mediterranean Basin. In addition, EU negotiators have retraced the steps of their American counterparts and ventured to South America and East Asia to open talks on consultative arrangements with the MERCOSUR (Argentina, Brazil, Paraguay, and Uruguay) and other Latin American countries as a first step toward substantive free-trade accords. They have also inaugurated an economic and political dialogue with Asia through the Asia Europe Meeting forum (ASEM).

This pursuit of regionalism by both sides has grated on the bilateral trade relationship in at least two ways. The first can be characterized as "attention diversion," which has to do with the priority that each side accords bilateral affairs in relation to trade with other partners and to participation in the multilateral trading system.[16]

The Americans worry that EU integration and enlargement will take precedence over WTO initiatives. In particular, the provision of regional preferences to prospective EU members in Central and Eastern Europe could reduce European interest in global liberalization. For one thing, WTO reforms, implemented on a most-favored-nation (MFN) basis, would dilute the value of the trade benefits accorded their potential partners. For another, MFN reforms would exacerbate adjustment pressures on EU firms that are already coping with single-market reforms and preferential access to the EU market by regional partners.

In turn, the Europeans worry about the diversion of U.S. attention to regional initiatives in Latin America and the Asia-Pacific region, which are home to the world's most rapidly growing economies. U.S. summits in those regions now overshadow those with European leaders, even though meetings between the U.S. president and European heads of state are more frequent. U.S. commitments to free trade with countries representing more than half of global output contrast markedly with the more limited reforms that the United States sought in the Uruguay Round and raise the specter of a two-bloc world in which the United States leads a far-flung group of high-growth, technologically dynamic nations versus a geographically compact bloc led by the European Union.

16. This concern has grown stronger, even though both sides have worked actively together since 1993 to complete the Uruguay Round, to pursue ongoing service sector negotiations in the WTO (the WTO Agreements on Basic Telecommunications and on Financial Services), and to spearhead the Information Technology Agreement (sealed at the WTO Singapore Ministerial in December 1996).

However, U.S. and EU problems entail more than attention-deficit disorders. The spread of regional arrangements by both sides increases the threat of discrimination against the trade of the other in each region. The United States has already filed several charges in the WTO because EU enlargement increased barriers to U.S. goods. Prospects for further expansion are equally worrying and, perhaps more important, raise questions about whether the European Union can sustain and augment its liberalization of agricultural protection.

Meanwhile, EU members fear that U.S. regional ventures will bring discrimination in the fast-growing Asia-Pacific region, as well as in important Latin American markets. Although APEC declarations have supported "open regionalism" and the multilateral trading system, few expect major APEC participants to give the European Union a free ride by implementing their free-trade commitments on an MFN basis. Without reciprocal EU liberalization (presumably in new WTO talks), EU firms would likely face discrimination. Recognizing that the United States had a viable alternative to the GATT if the Uruguay Round failed, EU officials responded positively to the APEC declaration on the Uruguay Round in November 1993, which offered to expand trade reforms to promote the completion of the GATT talks in December 1993.

To sum up, regional trade arrangements have generated only a handful of bilateral complaints over the past few decades, but new regional trade initiatives led separately by the United States and the European Union foreshadow increasing bilateral friction in the years ahead. This forecast is gloomy for the simple reason that both sides are pursuing more and larger agreements that discriminate against nonmembers and thus increase the risk of trade and investment diversion in high-growth emerging markets. Globalizing these regional free-trade commitments through new WTO initiatives would resolve these potential problems, although the realistic time horizon for multilateral action stretches well beyond the start of the new millennium.[17]

EUROPEAN MONETARY UNIFICATION. The second big issue left off the laundry list of trade complaints concerns the impact of European monetary unification on transatlantic trade. What impact will the policy reforms required to meet the Maastricht Treaty criteria have on economic growth, and therefore on the demand for traded goods? In

17. See Bergsten (1996).

other words, will EMU have a deflationary effect on European growth and thus reduce trade and investment opportunities? And will the convergence criteria encourage potential EMU partners to engage in competitive exchange rate depreciation during the transition to EMU (indeed, quite a bit has already happened in 1997), and to proffer state aid and increased trade protection to selectively counter the impact of changes in European currencies on their national industries—both of which could create a large bilateral trade surplus for Europe in its commerce with North America?

Trade ministers can do little to address these issues directly. However, they should consult closely with their colleagues in the finance ministries to ensure that transatlantic consultations in the G-7 and elsewhere fully consider the potential collateral damage to trading interests that could result from missteps in fiscal, monetary, exchange rate, and subsidy policies.

Parallel Approaches to Mitigate U.S.-EU Trade Frictions

As the preceding section indicates, the United States and the European Union need to address a host of bilateral trade issues in the coming years. Some are already the subject of bilateral discussions; others are under negotiation either bilaterally (for example, through mutual recognition agreements) or in multilateral fora such as the WTO (for example, public procurement) and the Organization for Economic Cooperation and Development (OECD, which hosts the ongoing talks on a multilateral agreement on investment, MAI).

Both sides resort to bilateral and multilateral negotiations as alternative (but not mutually exclusive) ways of resolving their conflicts. From the transatlantic interactions in both bilateral and multilateral fora, it appears that existing arrangements are adequate to the trade policy tasks at hand but are insufficient to resolve the broader foreign policy differences behind a few of the important bilateral disputes. This suggests three important lessons to guide the conduct of bilateral trade relations over the near to medium term.

Bilateral Approaches

U.S.-EU bilateral consultations cover a large and diverse set of issues. These discussions have been given higher priority since 1995 as a result of the work of the Transatlantic Business Dialogue (TABD). The TABD has developed an agenda of trade facilitation initiatives designed to feed proposals into the biannual meetings of U.S. and EU officials. Many of the proposals are similar to those put forward by business advisory groups in the APEC region.

Recommendations at the first meeting of the TABD in Seville in November 1995 led to the creation of fifteen advisory groups. Their function was to examine trade, tax, and regulatory issues and use the resulting information to help governments establish the Trans-Atlantic Marketplace (TAM) proposed at the U.S.-EU summit in December 1995. They were asked to develop proposals for removing barriers to transatlantic trade and investment in areas such as standards, certification, and regulatory policy; government procurement; intellectual property; and customs procedures. In essence, the business groups were asked to seek solutions to the problems they had highlighted in the trade barrier reports.

Particular attention was given to standards and certification practices with the dual aim of promoting convergence in regulatory procedures through the adoption of the principle "approved once, accepted everywhere," and the negotiation of mutual recognition agreements (MRAs) covering important sectors such as pharmaceuticals and medical devices. In addition, the TABD has urged the United States and European Union to join forces in promoting multilateral agreements in the WTO on both traditional and new trade issues, and laid the foundation for the successful conclusion of the ITA.

The ad hoc, results-driven approach of the TAM/TABD initiative has already produced tangible results. At the second meeting of the TABD in Chicago in November 1996, the two sides announced the completion of negotiations on an EU-U.S. Customs Cooperation and Mutual Assistance Agreement and the launching of a new transatlantic small-business initiative. In June 1997, after three years of negotiations, the European Union and the United States (and Canada) concluded mutual recognition agreements on inspection, testing, and certification procedures in pharmaceuticals, medical devices, telecommunications equipment, electromagnetic compatibility, electrical safety, and recreational craft.

By comparison, proposals for a Transatlantic Free Trade Agreement (TAFTA) are much less practical and actually could make current trade problems worse. This conclusion stems not from an ivory tower aversion to preferential trade arrangements (PTAs) but from sober analysis of the negotiating constraints and systemic risks that would likely result from such a pact.[18] Advocates believe that a TAFTA would require a relatively painless negotiation because of the low average level of existing barriers to bilateral trade and because agriculture (and other sensitive issues such as investment incentives) could be exempted from the free-trade obligations, as it has been in other PTAs negotiated by the European Union.

Contrary to these rosy projections, however, the negotiation of a TAFTA would face significant constraints and pose serious threats to the world trading system. In all likelihood, it will be difficult to liberalize tariff and nontariff barriers protecting certain sectors, even if the reforms are applied only to the transatlantic partners. Although such discrimination could be consistent with WTO obligations (if the conditions of GATT Article XXIV are met), the fact that the two richest regions discriminated against the rest of the world—and thus adversely affected the trade of developing countries—would clearly dampen prospects for further multilateral trade negotiations.

Furthermore, pushing farm trade problems under the rug will not make them go away, and differences over agriculture remain a key irritant in bilateral relations. In addition, a TAFTA would raise sensitive labor issues, since the pact would not simply link two high-wage labor regions but would encompass other countries with which the United States and the European Union engage in PTAs. In other words, negotiation of a TAFTA would be complicated by the ambiguity of the negotiating parties: that is to say, "Who is Us (U.S.)?" and "Who is Them (EU)"? Sir James Goldsmith was flatly wrong when he advocated a TAFTA as a rich man's club that would not have to worry about competition from low-wage sectors or economies. To isolate the trade of poorer regional partners from the TAFTA preferences, rules of origin would have to be constructed so as to create dense barriers to intraregional trade with U.S. and EU regional partners ranging from Mexico to Turkey, thereby undercutting the value of the PTAs now in place.

In sum, a TAFTA would yield minimal benefits if agriculture were excluded and would entail significant systemic costs if the liberaliza-

---

18. This argument draws on my more extensive critique of proposals for a TAFTA in Schott (1995).

tion were implemented on a discriminatory basis. If both sides agreed to extend their reforms on an MFN basis to all WTO members, it would make more sense to negotiate within the WTO, where other countries could undertake reciprocal liberalization in response to the U.S. and EU actions.

Multilateral Initiatives

The United States and the European Union have a long history of resolving bilateral trade problems in the context of multilateral trade negotiations. This trend has continued under the new WTO; in the future, bilateral disputes are even more likely to be brought to the WTO because its rights and obligations apply to a large share of trade in goods and services.

A substantial number of bilateral concerns already are being taken up in new WTO committees, negotiated in WTO fora, or prepped for future WTO negotiations mandated by the Uruguay Round accords (the so-called built-in agenda). For example, one of the first actions taken by the WTO in January 1995 was to establish a Committee on Trade and the Environment. The work of that committee includes discussions of issues that have been the focus of bilateral disputes: eco-labeling and the use of trade sanctions to enforce multilateral environmental agreements. In similar fashion, the WTO launched a new Committee on Regional Trade Agreements in late 1995 that aims to spotlight abuses of Article XXIV provisions that allow regional pacts to deviate from the GATT's MFN obligation.

The WTO has also concluded negotiations launched at the Uruguay Round on specific service sectors (basic telecommunications and finance services) and continued others (maritime services). In general, these talks target barriers to third-country markets of interest to both the United States and the European Union, but some specific bilateral problems were also on the negotiating agenda (such as regulatory/competition policies in basic telecommunications). In addition, the conclusion in March 1997 of the Information Technology Agreement promises to eliminate some relatively high EU tariffs.

Similarly, the WTO members have committed themselves to relaunching negotiations on agriculture and on overall trade in services by the end of the decade. These negotiations will revive efforts that yielded only marginal progress during past GATT rounds in lowering barriers to trade and constraining the use of domestic and export subsidies.

Both sides have worked together to broaden the WTO agenda to include issues that adapt the world trading rules to the new challenges arising from the increasing globalization of economic activity. Investment and competition policy top the list of issues in which working groups mandated by the Singapore Trade Ministerial in December 1996 will examine the need for and potential scope of prospective new WTO rights and obligations. WTO efforts on investment will complement negotiations already well under way on an MAI in the OECD and, it is hoped, will address the thorny issue of investment incentives, which has bedeviled bilateral relations for decades. Working in the OECD, the United States and Europe have signed a new pact on measures to limit corruption, especially in corporate competition for big public procurement contracts in countries such as China, India, and Brazil.

One bilateral dispute under review in the WTO that is not likely to be resolved concerns economic sanctions. Most sanctions are basically exempt from WTO disciplines because they are either mandated by the United Nations, applied against non-WTO countries, or justified under the national security provision of GATT Article XXI (which essentially affords a blank check for countries to pursue sanctions if they deem the measures to be in their national security interest).

For that reason, any WTO panels that may be constituted to review EU complaints will be highly unlikely to find that Helms-Burton or other sanctions laws abuse the Article XXI exemption. However, such panel reviews could well inflame political critics of the WTO, who will see the WTO cases as justification of their charges that WTO membership infringes national sovereignty and thus could undermine U.S. support for the WTO. To avoid that scenario, the United States has so far boycotted WTO review of Helms-Burton, and it is even mounting a vigorous defense of Massachusetts state-level sanctions that affect European firms doing business in Burma.

Conclusions

Transatlantic trade relations continue to be strong, with surprisingly few sources of friction, given the substantial two-way flows of trade and investment between the United States and the European

Union. Existing bilateral and multilateral initiatives already address the vast majority of problems of bilateral concern. The need is not for new channels of conflict resolution, but new strategies to strengthen domestic political support for the reforms required to remove obstacles to bilateral trade and investment in goods and services.[19]

The bilateral experience in dealing with the catalogue of trade conflicts and reform initiatives presented in this chapter yields three straightforward yet sublime lessons for the conduct of U.S.-EU trade relations:

— *If it ain't broke, don't fix it.* The current process of transatlantic cooperation, involving regular bilateral consultations as well as joint efforts in the OECD and the WTO (including its de facto steering group, the Quad), works well and needs few embellishments.

— *If you can't fix it, be careful not to break it.* Trade policy cannot cure all the ills of the transatlantic alliance. Both sides should take care to constrain trade responses to foreign policy disputes and macroeconomic imbalances. Such actions tend to inflame rather than soothe bilateral tensions.

— *Use the WTO to promote trade liberalization.* The WTO offers the best forum for dealing with current and nascent U.S.-EU trade frictions. Both sides should accelerate efforts to launch a comprehensive set of new trade talks in the WTO before the end of the decade. In contrast, bilateral initiatives such as TAFTA should be abandoned since they would likely conflict with WTO obligations by excluding sensitive sectors (and thus fail to mitigate trade tensions) or would generate political opposition at home to the required reforms.

19. See Schott (1996, chaps. 6, 7, and 15).

TABLE 3A-1. *U.S. Trade Complaints Regarding EU Trade Practices,*
1993–96[a]

Type of barrier	1993	1994	1995	1996
Import policies				
EU enlargement[b]	1	2	1	0
Customs classification[c]	0	0	1	1
Broadcast directive and motion picture quotas[d]	1	1	1	1
Agricultural and animal products[e]	10	8	6	6
Member state practices[f]	5	5	4	4
Standards, testing, labeling, and certification[g]				
Harmonized testing and certification[h]	1	1	1	1
Organic products[i]	1	1	0	0
Ban on hormone-treated meats[j]	1	1	1	1
Veterinary equivalency[k]	0	0	1	1
Ecolabeling scheme[l]	0	1	1	1
Member state practices[m]	2	4	5	5
Government procurement[n]				
Discrimination in the utilities sector[o]	1	1	1	1
Member state practices[p]	3	2	4	4
Export subsidies				
Agricultural export subsidies[q]	1	2	1	1
Canned fruit[r]	0	1	1	1
Intellectual property protection[s]	3	4	4	4
Member state practices[t]	6	8	7	10
Services barriers[u]	0	0	3	5
Member state practices[v]	2	3	3	3
Investment barriers[w]	2	2	4	4
Member state practices[x]	4	4	5	5
Other barriers[y]	6	7	5	5
Total	50	58	60	64

Source: USTR, *National Trade Estimate Report on Foreign Trade Barriers,* 1994, 1995,
1996, and 1997.

a. The annual reports present developments between April and March of the
previous year (for example, the 1994 report covers April 1993 to March 1994 and
is listed under the 1993 column).

b. EU enlargement to include Austria, Finland, and Sweden in January 1995 resulted in increased tariffs on U.S. exports. In accordance with WTO rules, the European Union negotiated a package of compensating tariff cuts. During the Uruguay
Round, the European Union agreed to permanently implement compensation—

TABLE 3A-1. *(continued)*

which it had provided to the United States since 1987—for the accession of Spain and Portugal to the European Union.

c. The European Commission's reclassification of products based on new computer technologies is a source of concern for the U.S. telecommunications equipment industry (see also *Inside US Trade,* May 24, 1996, p. 16).

d. The United States continues to monitor implementation of the 1989 quota provisions of the Broadcast Directive and has held consultations with the European Union under GATT Article XXII. The European Union remains on the Special 301 "priority watch list" because of this directive.

e. The United States continues to be concerned about the EU's reference price system for grains and rice, the EU's 1991 reclassification of corn gluten feed as mixed feed (which is subject to a higher import quota), import quotas on canned fish, restrictions affecting wine, a pending ban on fur from animals caught in leghold traps, and a new EU banana import regime. In 1993 and 1994 the United States was also concerned about the EU's Third Country Meat Directive and variable levies on agricultural goods; in 1993 softwood lumber import requirements and market access for U.S. whiskey were also areas of concern.

f. In addition to the EU Broadcast Directive, specific member states have implemented legislation that hinders the free flow of broadcast materials. These countries are France, Italy, Portugal, and Spain (and, previously, the United Kingdom).

g. Over the years, problems have tended to emerge from the evolution of the EU regulatory environment, including lags in the development of EU standards, lags in the drafting of harmonized legislation for regulated areas, inconsistent application and interpretation by member states of existing legislation, overlap among directives dealing with specific product areas, gray areas between the scope of various directives, and unclear marking and labeling requirements for these regulated products before they can be placed on the market.

h. The United States and the European Union are negotiating the resolution of differences in testing and certification procedures through mutual recognition agreements (MRAs). Discussions have been ongoing since 1992 and have been narrowed to focus on a few sectors including telecommunications, pharmaceuticals, and medical devices.

i. The U.S. concern relates to the EC requirement that organic products be certified by national bodies in the Community instead of relying on U.S. state and private certifications.

j. In 1989, the European Union banned imports of meat and meat products produced with growth-promoting hormones, which effectively eliminated most U.S. red meat product exports to the European Union. In response, the United States imposed 100 percent tariffs on imports of selected EU agricultural products, which remain in effect. In 1996 the United States requested WTO consultations with the European Union regarding the ban on hormone-treated meats.

k. The European Union does not recognize equivalent veterinary standards for livestock or livestock products from third countries. These products are subject to intermittent trade disruptions as negotiations on the matter continue.

TABLE 3A-1. *(continued)*

l. Consultations are in progress on the European Union's ecolabeling scheme, which has been listed as a "Super 301" program every year since 1994.

m. In addition to the issues listed above, the United States is concerned about the standards, testing, labeling restrictions, and certification requirements of five particular member states: Austria, France, Italy, Spain, and the United Kingdom.

n. In 1994 the United States and the European Union signed a bilateral government procurement agreement covering about $200 billion in public tenders (see Schott 1994, pp. 66–76).

o. Under the 1990 Utilities Directive, EU procuring utilities are permitted to exclude bids with less than 50 percent EU value. Moreover, acceptable bids with a majority of EU content must receive a 3 percent price preference over non-EU bids that are in all other respects equivalent. In May 1993 the United States and the European Union signed a bilateral agreement waiving some of the discriminatory provisions of the European Union's directive and the U.S. "Buy American" preferences and requirements. However, the United States simultaneously imposed sanctions on goods and services from certain EU member states in response to the European Union's refusal to eliminate discriminatory telecommunications procurement measures; the European Union responded in kind. In 1994 the United States and the European Union concluded the negotiation of a procurement agreement expanding upon the 1993 MOU, but did not end telecommunications discrimination. The telecommunications sanctions remain in force.

p. The national procurement practices of Denmark, Germany, Greece, Italy, and Spain have reportedly adversely affected U.S. exports.

q. U.S. concerns relate to the continued availability of EU agricultural export subsidies for a variety of products and to the implementation of a specific EU commitment to the United States to reduce oilseed subsidies.

r. The U.S. cling-peach industry remains concerned about the European Union's failure to enforce commitments made in the 1985 U.S.-EU Canned Fruit Agreement, in which the European Union agreed not to subsidize processing operations for peaches in syrup.

s. The United States continues to monitor EU intellectual property rights directives on software and the legal protection of designs, regulation of counterfeit goods and copyrights, patent filing and maintenance fees, and biotechnical inventions.

t. The United States is also concerned about member state practices pertaining to intellectual property protection. The United States monitors the levies collected on blank tapes and recording equipment in Belgium, France, Germany, and Spain. Greece has been on the Special 301 "watch list" since 1989 and the "priority watch list" since 1994, in large part because of rampant television piracy; in December 1996 Greece put forward an "action plan" of steps to be taken by April 1997. Italy has been "watch listed" under the Special 301 program since 1989, largely because of poor protection of copyrights for computer software and videos. The United Kingdom is being monitored for adherence to the TRIPs agreement, Sweden for lax enforcement of existing intellectual property rights laws, Germany for software piracy, and Ireland for its motion picture copyright law, which allegedly vi-

TABLE 3A-1. *(continued)*

olates the TRIPs agreement and EU directives. Spain's illegal "community video" systems are another area of concern. Austria's April 1996 amendment to its copyright law requiring statutory licenses for the exhibition of videos in hotels and other accommodations allegedly violates Austria's international obligations. And although the United States generally considers Denmark's intellectual property laws adequate, it is concerned that the Danish government does not provide provisional relief to prevent ongoing infringement, or preserve evidence for civil litigation, as required by the TRIPS agreement.

u. U.S. companies have complained about EU practices related to airline computer reservation services, ground-handling services at EU airports, and postal monopolies affecting express package services. In 1996 the United States grew concerned about EU proposals to allow member states to levy a value-added tax on foreign suppliers of telecommunications and online services. In January 1997 the European Union presented a new GATT schedule and MFN exemptions to accommodate EU enlargement to include Austria, Finland, and Sweden. The United States and other nations raised legal concerns that this draft document creates new opportunities for these three states to discriminate against service providers outside the European Union.

v. The United States continues to be concerned about legal services barriers in France, auditing barriers in Greece, and shipping restrictions in Spain.

w. Foreign investors in the European Union generally receive national treatment. However, the United States remains concerned over potential impediments to U.S. investment, including ownership restrictions in the aviation, maritime, satellite network, and communications industries; reciprocity provisions in financial services; the access to government grant programs of U.S. firms established in Europe; and OECD negotiations toward a Multilateral Agreement on Investment (MAI).

x. The United States remains concerned about investment barriers in five member states: Austria, France, Greece, Italy, and Portugal.

y. The United States continues to monitor French poultry regulations, EU subsidies to the shipbuilding industry (ratification of an OECD agreement is pending), and data transmission to non-EU countries. U.S. access to the telecommunications market is constrained by EU practices, though negotiations continue in the WTO on liberalizing basic telecommunications services. The United States is also concerned about government support for the European Airbus Consortium and continues to monitor compliance with the terms of the 1992 bilateral large aircraft agreement and the 1979 GATT Agreement on Trade in Civil Aircraft. In 1994 other areas of concern included Italian subsidies for engineering services and a moratorium on the use of Bovine Somatotrophin (BST). In 1993 the United States was concerned about developments related to standards, intellectual property, and competition policy in the European Telecommunications Standards Institute (ETSI).

TABLE 3A-2. *EU Trade Complaints Regarding U.S. Trade Practices,*
1993–96[a]

Type of barrier	1993	1994	1995	1996
Import policies				
Tariff barriers[b]	1	1	1	1
Customs reclassifications[c]	1	1	0	0
Customs user fees and excessive invoicing	2	2	2	2
Rules of origin[d]	0	0	0	1
Standards, testing, labeling, and certification				
State-level differences[e]	1	1	1	1
Nonuse of international standards[f]	1	1	2	1
Labeling requirements[g]	1	1	1	1
Excessive regulatory procedures[h]	1	1	1	1
Government procurement[i]	3	3	3	4
Antidumping/countervailing duties[j]	1	0	0	2
Intellectual property protection[k]	3	3	3	3
Service industries				
Financial services[l]	1	1	2	1
Professional services[m]	1	1	1	1
Maritime services[n]	3	3	3	3
Telecommunications and information[o]	4	4	5	5
Air transport and aeronautics[p]	4	4	4	5
Investment barriers				
Foreign ownership restrictions[q]	. . .	. . .	. . .	. . .
Conditional national treatment[r]	1	1	1	1
Other barriers				
Unilateralism[s]	3	3	3	3
Extraterritoriality[t]	5	5	6	6
National security[u]	4	4	4	4
Tax policy[v]	5	3	3	3
Agricultural and animal products[w]	9	6	6	6
Total	55	49	52	55

Source: European Commission, Report on United States Barriers to Trade and In-
vestment, 1994, 1995, 1996, and 1997.

a. The annual reports present developments between April and March of the
previous year (for example, the 1994 report covers April 1993 to March 1994 and
is listed under the 1993 column).

b. Despite Uruguay Round commitments, U.S. tariffs remain high in the textiles,
footwear, ceramics, glassware, leather goods, jewelry, truck, and railway car sectors.

TABLE 3A-2. *(continued)*

c. Several EU products (for example, sugar confectionery, red dye, and ivory cream marbles) were subject to increased tariffs as a result of their reclassification in the early 1990s. However, these tariff rates were reduced following the Uruguay Round.

d. In July 1996 the United States revised its rules of origin for textiles and clothing such that printing and dyeing no longer confer origin as before. In October 1996 the Italian textile industry filed a complaint under the Trade Barriers Regulation. Upon U.S. failure to make satisfactory proposals to solve the problem, the European Union requested WTO consultations on the matter in May 1997.

e. The European Union cites examples of differences between federal and state-level standards, such as California regulations affecting lead content in ceramic ware, safe drinking water, and the percentage of recovered glass in recycled glass bottles.

f. U.S. preference for U.S. standards and the lack of awareness of international standards continue to be problems for EU exporters to the United States. Illustrative cases include the 1990 Fastener Quality Act, which imposes different testing requirements than those set internationally under ISO 9000 standards; and the 1990 Nutrition Labeling and Education Act, which requires certain products to be labeled with their content and origin, which differs from international standards on labeling established by the Codex Alimentarius. In 1995 the European Union intervened in support of Brazil and Venezuela's WTO complaint regarding U.S. legislation affecting reformulated and conventional gasoline; in January 1996 the WTO dispute settlement panel decided that the U.S. Gasoline Rule was a violation of national treatment obligations under the GATT. The EPA is currently revising U.S. requirements for gasoline imports.

g. For example, wine labeling must be approved at the federal level and the state level; sometimes this takes as much as four and a half months for approval.

h. The European Union is concerned about the heavy regulatory approach of the United States: for example, third-party intervention in the regulatory process and the concentration of certification authority in the hands of U.S. agencies, particularly the Food and Drug Administration.

i. Despite the U.S.-EU agreement on government procurement concluded during the Uruguay Round, the European Union remains concerned about federal and state "Buy American" legislation, procurement in the telecommunications sector, and the federal set-aside program for small businesses, which close off procurement opportunities to foreign firms. In June 1996 the Commonwealth of Massachusetts enacted legislation forbidding state agencies and authorities from entering contracts with firms doing business with or located in Burma, in an effort to support human rights. This and similar measures proposed in other states allegedly violate the GPA by limiting the access of European suppliers to those states. The European Union requested WTO consultations on June 20, 1997.

j. In 1993 the United States imposed CVDs on a significant portion of the EU's steel exports to the U.S. market, allegedly more than offsetting the competition-distorting effect of subsidies and therefore erecting a new trade barrier. In July

TABLE 3A-2. *(continued)*

1996 the U.S. Department of Commerce imposed CVDs on pasta from Italy to countervail EC export refunds for cereals used in manufacturing pasta, allegedly violating item 8 of the U.S.-EC Pasta Settlement of 1987. In addition, the 1916 Anti-Dumping Act's prohibition of the import or sale of foreign products at less than market value allegedly violates the GATT and the Anti-Dumping Agreement. The European Union has raised this issue before the WTO Anti-Dumping Commission; the examination procedure began in February 1997.

k. The European Union is concerned about the first-to-invent approach of U.S. patent law, patent infringement immunities for U.S. government agencies, and copyright protection to third-country works (films, books). These issues were covered by the WTO TRIPs agreement, and the European Union is concerned about U.S. implementation of its Uruguay Round commitments.

l. U.S. sectoral segmentation rules (for example, the Glass Steagall Act) block the establishment of global integrated financial services organizations and discriminate against foreign-controlled banks, especially at the state level. In 1995 the European Union also expressed concern about U.S. nonparticipation in the July 1995 GATT financial services negotiations.

m. Licensing of professional (legal and accounting) services at the state level is not transparent or open.

n. The European Union is concerned about subsidies and tax policies for the U.S. shipbuilding industry and cargo preferences for U.S.-flag vessels.

o. The European Union has long been concerned about U.S. reciprocity-based licensing procedures, investment restrictions related to Section 310 of the 1934 Communications Act, the Federal Communication Commission's broad powers, and export controls on encryption products. In November 1995 the United States introduced equivalency tests for foreign carriers, raising an additional concern. Although U.S. encryption controls were eased somewhat in late 1996 and early 1997, the European Union feels they still represent a substantial barrier.

p. The European Union is concerned about discriminatory practices linked to the U.S. computer reservation systems, foreign ownership restrictions of air carriers, drug and alcohol programs required for all air carriers operating in the United States, and subsidies to the U.S. aeronautics industry. In April 1996 the United States enacted the Hatch Amendment, requiring the Federal Aviation Administration to apply national security measures to foreign air carriers, allegedly breaching international agreements.

q. Foreign ownership restrictions are included in telecommunications and information and air transport and aeronautics.

r. The European Union is concerned about recent U.S. legislation related to cross-sectoral reciprocity and performance requirements in research and development, technology programs, financial services, and antitrust exposure of production joint ventures.

s. The European Union is concerned about unilateralism in U.S. trade legislation to the extent that unilateral sanctions or retaliatory measures take place without reference to, or in defiance of, agreed multilateral trade rules. The Euro-

TABLE 3A-2. *(continued)*

pean Union monitors actions pursuant to Section 301, Super 301, and Special 301 of U.S. trade legislation. The European Union was particularly concerned in 1994 with U.S. sanctions imposed as a result of the EU's ban on hormone-treated livestock, an extension of the retaliation list to Dutch veal, complaints against the EU's banana regime, and U.S. procurement sanctions based on Title VII of the 1988 Omnibus Trade and Competitiveness Act. In 1993 the European Union was also concerned about Super 301-analogous provisions of the U.S. Telecommunications Trade Act of 1988.

t. The European Union has complained about the following measures, all of which are applicable outside U.S. territory: sanctions against foreign nationals and companies investing or trading in petroleum and natural gas–related technologies with Iran and Libya (the 1995 Iran Oil Sanctions Act), the trade embargo against Cuba (for example, the 1996 Libertad Act and the 1992 Cuban Democracy Act), product liability law that gives U.S. courts jurisdiction over manufacturers based outside the United States, the tuna-dolphin law (which allows sanctions to be imposed against countries that fail to apply similar standards for dolphin protection), threats of a shrimp embargo of countries whose shrimp fishermen cannot provide evidence of their attempts to match U.S. sea turtle protection, and consent rights over reprocessing, enrichment, and storage of nuclear material.

u. The European Union is concerned that restrictions to trade and investment based on national security mask protectionist intent. Concerns have been raised regarding import restrictions based on Section 232, unilateral determinations of export controls and licenses, procurement restrictions (for example, the Berry Amendment), and investment and foreign ownership restrictions (for example, the Exon-Florio amendment and the Jones Act).

v. The European Union continues to be concerned about cumbersome and discriminatory U.S. information reporting requirements, arbitrarily calculated state corporate income taxes, and "earnings stripping" provisions that limit the extent to which interest payments can be deducted from taxable income, and it was previously concerned about tax discrimination against imported (European) cars and discriminatory beer and wine excise taxes until these measures were removed.

w. Complaints related to agricultural and animal products are numerous. The European Union has expressed concern about programs that subsidize or promote exports of U.S. agricultural products, marketing loans for agricultural commodities, tariff rate quotas applied to cheese and other dairy products, sanitary and phytosanitary restrictions on numerous products (including hormones), domestic content requirements for tobacco, cotton import fees, inadequate protection for geographical indications of European wine, unilateral determinations on drift-net fishing, and allocations to foreign fishing fleets. In 1994 following a GATT panel ruling that U.S. domestic content requirements for tobacco contravened Article III of the GATT, the United States expressed its intention to remove the provisions and began negotiations with the European Union.

Chapter 4

European Monetary Unification and International Monetary Cooperation

Barry Eichengreen and Fabio Ghironi

Monetary affairs are not a leading sphere of cooperation between the Europe and the United States. Were bilateral issues ranked by the extent of concerted and sustained cooperation, interest rate and exchange rate policies would surely rank behind security, financial market regulation, and trade. Still, monetary cooperation between Europe and the United States and among the central banks and governments of the Group of Seven (G-7) has played a significant role on occasion, as it did when the dollar soared in the mid-1980s and slumped in 1994 and during exceptional crises such as the Mexican meltdown of 1994–95 and the Asian crisis of 1997–98.

European monetary unification is likely to discourage even modest initiatives such as these. The European Central Bank (ECB) will assume the tasks of the national central banks of those European states that participate in the monetary union. The Council of Ministers (in consultation with the ECB, the European Commission, and the European Parliament) will make decisions regarding European participation in any new global exchange rate arrangement. Policymakers in Europe and elsewhere are understandably preoccupied with how these bodies will manage the monetary affairs of the newly formed Euro zone and are paying less attention to the implications for cooperation with the rest of the world.

Thanks go to Gary Hufbauer, Andrew Moravcsik, Robert Powell, and participants in the Council on Foreign Relations Study Group on Transatlantic Relations for their helpful comments and to Kira Reoutt for editorial assistance.

Meanwhile, many American officials remain blissfully ignorant of the entire process.

This is unfortunate, for there is some reason to think that economic and monetary union will in fact increase the need for international monetary cooperation. Any liquidation by the ECB of the excess dollar reserves it inherits from national central banks will disturb the foreign exchange market. Inasmuch as exchange market stability is a shared priority of Europe and the United States, such disturbances may invite concerted intervention and other forms of international monetary cooperation.

This chapter describes some of the opportunities and perils for international monetary cooperation associated with EMU. Our approach brings together two strands in the literature, one concerned with institutions and the other focusing on policy consensus.[1] Institutions merit attention because they play an important role in all such cooperation. Despite an awareness that their monetary policies spill over to the rest of the world and that policy trades may be mutually advantageous, countries may still find cooperating difficult in the absence of an adequate institutional framework. Institutions are required to overcome the transaction, implementation, and monitoring costs that otherwise impede coordination and collective action and frustrate the best intentions of officials. Institutions can thus encourage international cooperation even when they lack enforcement power.

The connections between policy consensus and international policy coordination are equally important. Strictly speaking, policymakers do not have to share a common outlook in order to implement a coordinated set of policies. One can imagine physicians prescribing a common course of treatment even when they diagnose different illnesses or hold different views of how a medicine works. Such coincidences are, however, likely to be rare. Officials have to justify their

---

1. Although the literature on the roles of both institutions and ideas in international cooperation is vast, the topics tend to be treated separately. The closest approximation to the approach presented in this chapter is found in Goldstein (1988). However, Goldstein focuses on trade rather than monetary policy and on domestic rather than international institutions. Private sector preferences should also figure in any discussion of monetary policy; although they feature in the account that follows, they are not the focus of the analysis. Henning (1994), in another study with points of contact with this chapter, stresses the role of domestic institutions in building domestic consensus. Our argument can be thought of as an international counterpart to his.

actions to different domestic constituencies (just as physicians must justify the course of treatment to different family members), and the credibility of their rationale may be called into question if they do so in conflicting ways. A shared diagnosis and prescription may therefore be needed to coordinate monetary policy internationally.[2]

In fact, the roles of institutionalization and consensus formation in international monetary cooperation are related. Institutions, by providing a venue for the ongoing, systematic exchange of information and ideas, foster consensus formation. They serve an agenda-setting function that gives precedence to certain conceptual formulations above others. Expert analyses further define the terms of discourse and decisionmaking. The written record and recollections of permanent staff allow these processes to endure beyond the terms in office of any particular set of elected officials.

The tendency for policy consensus to encourage institution building works in reciprocal fashion. Just as physicians who share a common view of threats to public health are most likely to agree on the equipment needed in hospitals and on the structure of diagnostic services, monetary policymakers who share a common model of the threats to financial stability are most likely to agree on the appropriate institutional response. Thus an emerging consensus in the 1960s that international monetary cooperation was stymied by the inadequate resources of the International Monetary Fund led to the creation of the General Arrangements to Borrow, which in turn encouraged the formalization of the Group of Seven and Group of Ten (G-10) and regular summits of finance ministers and central bankers from the industrial countries. Recognition that the balance of payments adjustment process was not working smoothly led to the creation of Working Party 3 of the Economic Policy Committee of the Organization for Economic Cooperation and Development. These examples illustrate the role of consensus formation in institutionalizing the policy-coordination process.

Insofar as institutions and consensus affect one another in mutually reinforcing ways—with institutions encouraging consensus and

---

2. Whereas we emphasize the existence of barriers to sharing and processing information, a related literature (for example, Morrow 1994) focuses on the incentive of governments concerned with the international distribution of the gains to withhold information as a way of garnering a larger share of the international gains.

consensus facilitating institution building—the system they constitute will produce positive feedback. A characteristic of such systems is that outcomes are sensitive to initial conditions. Passing shocks are able to affect institutions, consensus, and policy practices in permanent ways. Technically, these conditions can give rise to multiple equilibria and historical path dependence.[3] The implication is that history matters for international monetary cooperation.

The discussion therefore opens with an account of the history of international monetary cooperation, to illustrate the roles of institutions and expert consensus.[4] As past experience shows, cooperation has been most successful when it has been most institutionalized and where the greatest consensus has prevailed. These conditions have been more prevalent in Europe than elsewhere in the industrial world. Although the coordination of monetary policy in Europe has been far from perfect (the aftermath of German unification illustrates the point), it has been more extensive and systematic than in the bilateral dealings of Europe and the United States.

Our analysis raises questions about the scope for monetary cooperation in Europe and across the Atlantic. Although institutional and intellectual support for coordinating monetary policy within Europe will be further strengthened in Stage III of the transition to EMU, that framework has limitations concerning relations between the "ins" and the "outs," that is, between member states that will and will not be founding members of the monetary union. Although this problem can be remedied, at present it is a threat to monetary cohesion in Europe and to the broader program of political integration with which the EMU project is linked. Moreover, institutional and intellectual support for transatlantic cooperation, and for G-7 cooperation more generally, remains weak. In recent years, interest has begun to shift from the coordination of monetary policy to the management of financial crises. The Mexican crisis of 1994–95 revealed gaps in the in-

3. See Arthur (1988).
4. The constraints of space necessarily limit the scope of our treatment. We focus on European motives and capacities for engaging in international monetary cooperation since it is in Europe that the most dramatic changes are taking place. We say less about the United States and even less about Japan. But the full implications of European Monetary Union can only be grasped within the framework of international monetary cooperation provided by global institutions such as the International Monetary Fund, the Bank for International Settlements, and annual Group of Seven summits. Hence, these arrangements also figure in the discussion that follows.

stitutional framework available for dealing with such problems, and in its wake important innovations have taken place. But here, too, as the subsequent Asian crisis illustrates, more remains to be done.

Institutions and Intellectual Consensus

In this section we describe problems of commitment and coordination that thwart efforts at monetary cooperation and suggest how institutions help to overcome those obstacles. We highlight the role of intellectual consensus in policy action and specify the linkages between institutionalization and consensus formation.

The Problems for Cooperation

The spillover effects of monetary policies and the welfare gains from policy coordination have been amply discussed in the literature.[5] Paradoxically, in real life the international coordination of monetary policies has been the exception, not the rule.[6] This, it would appear, is the peculiar case of a free lunch, in that there exist significant unexploited welfare gains for the countries concerned.

But policy coordination also carries costs, and these can be large when coordination takes place in an ad hoc manner.[7] First, it can be costly to *assemble the information needed to coordinate policies*. A mutually advantageous policy mix is impossible to arrive at without information on monetary and economic conditions in the countries that are party to the agreement. Monetary policymakers often operate behind a veil of ignorance: their decisions are based on incomplete information about the strength of the economy, and they have even less information on its prospective strength six to nine months from now when the effects of monetary initiatives are felt. Such information is especially poor when it comes to foreign economic conditions.

Second, it is costly to *evaluate the connections between policy and eco-*

5. International coordination can be thought of as moving to a situation in which the international externalities associated with national policies are internalized. A good introduction to the relevant literature appears in Bryant and others (1988).

6. See, for example, Cooper and others (1989) and Henning (1994).

7. These "costs" should not be interpreted too literally; the factors we discuss can be thought of, more generally, as obstacles to international policy coordination, following Frankel (1988). Much of our discussion of the topic draws on this useful work.

nomic conditions. Officials may not all understand, much less agree on, how policy affects the economy (whether a change in monetary conditions affects mainly inflation or growth, for example). These problems are especially severe in the international domain, where the cross-border effects of monetary policy are a matter of serious concern.

Third, it can be costly to *reach a consensus on the impact of policy adjustments.* Policymakers are unlikely to agree on mutually advantageous policy trades when they favor different economic models.[8] In the presence of uncertainty, officials will not be inclined to strike a bargain unless they expect to gain under the models espoused by both governments. This suggests that bargaining will not even start unless both countries have such expectations.[9] Since it is not likely that both countries will gain under both models, disagreements in this area are a major obstacle to cooperation. Hence it may not be possible to reach a consensus without protracted negotiations, which themselves are likely to entail significant costs.[10]

Fourth, it may be costly to *implement policy adjustments.* Few events draw more financial and political attention than changes in monetary policy. If implementation is to be effective, public opinion must be swayed to ensure a favorable reception.[11] International coordination means moving domestic policy in a direction that is undesirable when taken in isolation; the adverse effects are then more than counterbalanced by the beneficial impact of changes in policy abroad. Public opinion will be difficult to influence under such circumstances. In addition, it may be necessary to implement adjustments in domestic and foreign policies simultaneously so as to impress the public with the linkage.

Fifth, the costs of *monitoring compliance* can be substantial. Typically, each country adjusts policy in a way that is undesirable in isolation but is then more than compensated by the adjustment of policy abroad. Countries will have an incentive to renege on this bargain if they can avoid being caught (since the government would obtain the adjustment in foreign policies it desires without any compromise of

---

8. Frankel and Rockett (1988).

9. See Holtham and Hughes-Hallett (1987); Kenen (1990).

10. This issue of consensus formation is a key element of our argument; we return to it below.

11. Readers need only recall the 1994–95 Mexican crisis for an illustration of the point.

its own policy stance). The longer the lag between a country's defection and its partners' reversion to noncooperative behavior, the greater the incentive to renege. Thus, effective monitoring will help to support cooperation.

Sixth, it can be costly to *enforce the agreement*. If the only recourse available to the partners of a country that cheats is to withdraw their cooperation, they may be reluctant to agree to the bargain in the first place. If the agreement breaks down quickly, countries will have sunk the costs just outlined without reaping compensating benefits. Before deciding to cooperate, they may therefore demand sanctions to reduce the incentive to renege. In practice, however, it may be impractical to develop an enforcement technology with penalties for countries that back down on the agreement.

In the real world, the nature of the economic problem, the policy stance, and the direction of cross-border spillovers may not even be evident to the initiating country, much less to its foreign partners. Assuming that governments can pool the relevant information at no cost misses much of the action. Add to this the problems of implementation and enforcement, and the obstacles to cooperation can be significant.

Mechanisms for Cost Containment and Consensus Formation

The institutions of international monetary cooperation—the International Monetary Fund (IMF), Working Party 3, G-7 Summits, and the Monetary Committee of the European Union—can be considered mechanisms for reducing these costs. Such institutions are able to centralize the gathering of information and thus reduce the cost of this activity, whereas different governments working in parallel end up duplicating one another's efforts. Examples of this centralizing can be seen at the IMF, in its assembling of statistics on the balance of payments and government finance; at the OECD, in the issuing of its "main economic indicators"; and at the European Monetary Institute and European Commission, in the publishing of their "convergence indicators."

A central function of IMF surveillance, OECD country studies, and the directorates of the European Commission is to assess the spillovers of policy across borders. Small countries in particular may not have the expertise needed to analyze the connections between policies abroad and conditions at home; this is where an international organization may be said to have a comparative advantage.

The institutionalized exchange of information and views can help countries arrive at a consensus. The regular meetings of Working Party 3, G-7 Summits, the IMF Executive Board, the BIS, and the Committee of Central Bank Governors of the European Union do more than simply encourage the flow of ideas. Meetings provide precedents, past agendas shape future agendas, staff analyses provide terms of reference, and statistics reported in background reports direct the attention of officials to important policy problems. An institution's written records and the collective memory of its staff lend continuity to a process that would otherwise be disrupted by changes in government administration.

As already explained, cooperation cannot take place without mechanisms for implementing policy adjustments and monitoring compliance. Institutions supply these measures. The Monetary Committee of the European Union, for example, has standard procedures for negotiating realignments of ERM currencies and supporting currencies under pressure. Another EU institution, the Commission, is empowered by the Maastricht Treaty to work with the Monetary Committee in monitoring countries' compliance with their monetary, fiscal, and exchange rate commitments. The treaty also authorized the creation of the European Monetary Institute to cultivate a consensus regarding the implementation of monetary policy and to harmonize the institutional arrangements of the prospective national participants in EMU. It provides for sanctions against countries that fail to adhere to the bargain: in Stage II of the Maastricht process, a country violating the treaty's Excessive Deficit Procedure may be barred from the monetary union; in Stage III, the Council could require the member state in question to publish additional information before issuing bonds and securities, may invite the European Investment Bank to "reconsider" its lending policy toward the country, may require that country to make non-interest-bearing deposits with the Community, and may impose fines.

Other Views on Mechanisms for Coordination

A variety of opinions exist on the best mechanism for coordination. Political scientists working on international regimes suggest that monitoring and sanctioning benefit above all from the repeated inter-action of countries, through the collective oversight and enforcement that such interaction permits.[12] Economists who study international policy coordination, and specifically the possibilities and effects of cooperation when policymakers disagree on the basic economic model, tend to emphasize the gains from consultation and informa-tion exchange, including consultations designed to reconcile analyti-cal frameworks.[13]

Similarly, economists who study communication networks empha-size the role that such networks can play in reducing the costs of in-formation processing and transmission.[14] When it takes time to absorb information, because the flow is too large to be processed in its entirety by any one individual or set of agents, the amount spent on absorbing it can be reduced if agents specialize in processing par-ticular types of information.[15] To this end, several individuals could form a team (or, in the context of industrial organization, a firm). Since the costs of such processing make it optimal for agents to as-similate less than all the information available, they introduce bounded rationality and therefore a role for institutions.[16]

12. Keohane (1983). Although Keohane also discusses the role of institutions in dis-seminating information and reducing transactions costs, we move beyond his analysis by "unpacking" the functions of the institutions of international monetary cooperation.

13. See, for example, Bryant (1987), Horne and Masson (1988). But they do not focus, as we do here, on institutions as mechanisms for facilitating consultation and informa-tion exchange.

14. See Bolton and Dewatripont (1994).

15. Time can be thought of as a metaphor for costs of information processing generally.

16. One can imagine how it can be similarly costly for governments to process infor-mation about economic conditions and policies in foreign countries. In this case, the specialized information-processing and dissemination services required to enhance communication can be lodged with an international organization with a constituency large enough to support a range of such specialized services. The size of that institution would be determined, as in Bolton and Dewatripont (1994), by the trade-off between the returns to specialization and the costs of communication (since additional specialization entails additional communication and hence additional costs). This approach shares with ours the assumption that policymakers face costs of processing and transmitting information. It provides a rationale for the existence of a centralized organization (in our context, an international institution). But, we are inclined to interpret the informa-tion advantages of institutionalization more broadly than Bolton and Dewatripont. In their framework, institutionalization permits teamwork and specialization. We would argue in addition that institutionalization reduces communication costs by providing a structure for discussions, by generating documents that serve as points of reference, and by encouraging the development of a common analytical language.

The literature on epistemic communities emphasizes yet another mechanism for cooperation: "networks of professionals with recognized expertise and competence in a particular domain and an authoritative claim to policy-relevant knowledge."[17] These experts are a source of information and knowledge that can help policymakers overcome the uncertainties they face by lending credence to particular interpretations of phenomena.[18] In this way, they are able to guide policymakers toward shared formulations and common characterizations of the linkages between policies and outcomes.[19]

Recent Experience with International Monetary Cooperation

In this section we analyze in more detail the role of institutions in facilitating the coordination of monetary policies, reviewing industrial-country experience generally before focusing on the European case. We argue that more extensive institutionalization and policy consensus have supported more systematic monetary policy coordination in this region than elsewhere in the advanced industrial world.

Transatlantic Monetary Cooperation from Bretton Woods to Today

When the International Monetary Fund was conceived at Bretton Woods in July 1944, a primary concern of the framers was to prevent

17. Haas (1992, p. 3).

18. The point can be illustrated in the context of international monetary cooperation and the construction of international monetary institutions by the role of U.S. and British economic experts in the Bretton Woods negotiations, as analyzed by Ikenberry (1993).

19. This approach shares with the preceding one the assumption of bounded rationality, insofar as it suggests that policymakers are unable to comprehend the connections between policy instruments and targets on their own. However, we emphasize not the superior analytical ability of experts, but rather the tendency for institutions to channel the discussions and discourse through which policy officials themselves arrive at a consensus. The obstacle to cooperation may not be the inability of policymakers to formulate "models" of the connection between instruments and targets, but rather their inability to agree on the applicability of any one model to the problem at hand. Institutionalized procedures and structures, besides allowing expert analysis to lend legitimacy to some models above others, makes certain models the point of departure for discussions.

a recurrence of the competitive devaluations and beggar-thy-neighbor monetary policies of the 1930s. Their goal was to create a mechanism for consultation and collaboration on monetary problems.[20] But this idea was soon overshadowed by disputes over the structure of the Fund and over the power it should have to influence the domestic policies of its members. The only explicit obligations members were charged with under the Articles of Agreement were to maintain the par values of their currencies and restore current account convertibility after a transitional period. With the advent of IMF conditionality in the 1950s, Fund credit came with stipulations that sometimes took into account the foreign repercussions of domestic policies, but the conditions seldom made mention of international policy coordination. In fact, the industrial countries were reluctant to subject themselves to IMF oversight. Restricting exchange rate adjustments to episodes of fundamental disequilibrium rendered that step and associated consultations with the Fund an embarrassing admission of policy failure.

The restoration of current account convertibility in 1958 made clear the inadequacy of existing mechanisms for policy coordination. Working Party 3 of the Economic Policy Committee of the OECD was a response to this institutional lacuna.[21] It was designed to encourage dialogue on policies affecting balance of payments adjustment, which had emerged by the 1960s as a principal problem afflicting the Bretton Woods System. The members of Working Party 3—deputy ministers, and deputy central bank governors of the leading industrial countries (along with the OECD Secretariat and representatives of other international institutions)—met every six to eight weeks to discuss the impact of domestic policies on other countries.

The OECD provided them with background documentation, forecasts, and analyses of national economic conditions. More important, it responded to the demand from Working Party 3 and the Group of Ten countries (the advanced industrial nations that underwrote the General Arrangements to Borrow) for a more systematic framework

20. In the words of the Articles, the purpose of the Fund was "to promote international monetary cooperation through a permanent institution which provides the machinery for consultation and collaboration on international monetary problems."

21. Two useful accounts of the history of Working Party 3 are Crockett (1989) and Schoorl (1995).

for the formulation of balance of payments policies. The result was a landmark report acknowledging that policy coordination should extend beyond monitoring whether countries were complying with their obligation to maintain par values and current account convertibility.[22] It encouraged the regular exchange of information on national policies and economic conditions, emphasized the analysis of the compatibility of national forecasts, and recommended the development of an "early warning system" to signal incipient payments problems. These functions are akin to the information exchange, monitoring, and consensus formation described earlier in the chapter as key roles of institutions.

But balance of payments diplomacy in the second half of the 1960s was beset by problems that discouraged countries from forming a consensus. In particular, U.S., French, and German policymakers held different views on the sources of the American balance of payments deficit and hesitated to reveal their true willingness to adjust in order to persuade their foreign counterparts to bear the bulk of the adjustment burden. Furthermore, institutional support for information exchange, monitoring, and consensus formation did not extend to implementation and enforcement.[23]

When the Bretton Woods system broke down—some say because the United States failed to take into account the systemic repercussions of its policies—an opportunity arose to extend the institutional framework. The initiatives that were considered emphasized information exchange, monitoring, and consensus formation. In 1976 the interim committee agreed on a new Article IV of the IMF's charter instructing the Fund to exercise "firm surveillance" of national policies and to develop principles for policy formulation (in a faint echo of Bretton Woods, it also called on countries to maintain stable exchange rates and to refrain from manipulating their currencies). As a step toward institutionalization, the Executive Board began to hold

22. Working Party 3 (1966). Although this report focused on the sustainability of individual countries' balance of payments positions rather than the implications for their industrial-country partners and systemic stability, it was a significant step toward a framework for more systematic international policy coordination.

23. IMF stand-by arrangements in the upper credit tranches became increasingly prevalent in the second half of the 1960s, and these created at least one mechanism with financial carrots attached to encourage the implementation of these principles. As before, however, IMF programs were mainly directed at developing countries, not toward the industrial economies.

regular discussions of the IMF's *World Economic Outlook,* which offered staff analyses of the global impact of national economic policies. Other forms of institutionalization included increasingly comprehensive and regular consultations with governments under the aegis of Article IV, special consultations with countries whose policies had the potential to create problems for their neighbors or the international system, and an "information notice system" alerting the Executive Board to and providing staff analysis of exceptional currency fluctuations.

While a step forward, Article IV surveillance suffered from the same limitations as the Working Party 3 initiative. Information exchange, monitoring, and expert analysis were necessary but not sufficient to ensure consensus formation, as became evident in the 1980s when countries could not agree on the causes of the dollar's fluctuation or the debt and financial difficulties of the developing countries. Governments had a familiar incentive to withhold information about their interpretation of events and their willingness to adjust in the hope that their foreign counterparts would be forced to assume the greatest part of the adjustment burden. In the absence of enforcement power, even course corrections on which policy officials agreed were difficult to implement. Hence there was no comprehensive, coordinated policy response to either problem.

Those problems did, however, cause concern about the limitations of the prevailing framework. Another report by the Group of Ten, this one published in the mid-1980s, again advocated strengthened surveillance and peer pressure to encourage consistent policies. But cooperation was limited. Policy coordination, when it occurred, was an ad hoc reaction and was restricted to exchange rate support, as was the case at the time of the Plaza and Louvre accords and during subsequent episodes of concerted intervention on behalf of the dollar, most recently in April 1995.

The fact that disputes over the effectiveness of the Plaza and Louvre accords persisted indicates that their impact was far from overwhelming. The problem was that governments were reluctant to follow through with changes in domestic policies, especially in regard to fiscal matters, and no mechanism was in place to compel them to do so. Furthermore, they were unable to commit central banks to sustained shifts in monetary policy. The only instrument available was sterilized intervention. Without a commitment to adjust domestic policies, such intervention had limited effects at best. In the end, these efforts foundered in the absence of an institutional mechanism to compel domestic policy adjustments.

Nevertheless, a modest advance was made when it was decided to issue regular communiqués following G-7 summits and ministerial meetings.[24] In drafting communiques, countries were encouraged to exchange information and seek a consensus, although the substantive content of the communiques, and therefore the pressure for policy change, varied. When a consensus was not reached, as with the causes of the "twin deficits" of the United States in the 1980s, communiques tended to be vague. The agreement at the 1986 Tokyo Summit to rely on an explicit set of economic indicators, for example, failed to specify exactly what indicators should be considered and what to do with them.[25] A similar problem arose with the Interim Committee's 1987 declaration that national economic policies should be gauged in terms of their "desirability" and "sustainability."

Another striking example of the advantages and limitations of institutionalized cooperation can be found in the Mexican rescue of 1994. Although the IMF and G-10 had designed mechanisms, namely stand-by arrangements and the General Arrangements to Borrow (GAB), to cope with this situation, the Fund was unable to operate on the requisite scale or with the necessary speed. Members of its Executive Board had to consult with their governments, and this took time. Having failed to reach a common diagnosis of the crisis, U.S. and European governments could not come together on a response. Though the GAB was the obvious source for augmenting the Fund's financial resources, support for a noncontributor (Mexico) could only take place, in the words of the arrangement, in an "exceptional situation of a character or aggregate size that could threaten the stability of the international monetary system." Officials were unable to determine whether Mexico satisfied this condition in the short period the markets gave them to respond. As a result, the crisis required exceptional action by the United States and the IMF.[26]

24. The IMF took part in these exercises from the 1980s, providing statistical and analytical input.

25. For further discussion of this history, see Frankel (1990).

26. Whether management of future crises will be more effective is an open question. Steps are under way to better institutionalize the Fund's capacity to manage financial crises in emerging markets; these are described later in the chapter.

European Exceptionalism

The European economies are relatively open and trade disproportionately with one another. They are sensitive to the cross-border spillovers of national policies, having experienced the disruptions associated with competitive devaluation in the 1930s. Hence after World War II they were quick to develop structures for encouraging monetary policy coordination; these structures evolved into the monetary institutions of the European Union.

The organization of European nations that eventually came to be known as the OECD (previously named the CEEC and the OEEC) was established in response to the Marshall Plan. When the United States insisted that recipients cooperate in the allocation of U.S. aid, it became necessary to reconcile forecasts of unfinanced current account deficits to see that these did not exceed the aid on offer, and policies had to be adjusted accordingly. The European Payments Union (EPU), the clearing system established in 1950, was a direct descendent of the Marshall Plan. The task of monitoring national policies and recommending adjustments was entrusted to the EPU's Managing Board, which was made up of experts seconded by participating countries reporting to the Council of the OEEC. To obtain exceptional EPU credits, countries had to accept the Managing Board's policy conditionality and report monthly on their progress.

With the resumption of current account convertibility, the OECD was expanded to include the United States. The smaller European countries insisted that its Working Party 3 should retain the same membership structure as the EPU Managing Board. This institutional continuity lent structure and coherence to its deliberations.[27]

The desire for closer policy coordination reflected the need to pursue European integration as a strategy for locking Germany into Europe and the need to insulate European monetary affairs from unpredictable U.S. policy.[28] The Treaty of Rome acknowledged that exchange rates and macroeconomic policies were matters of "common concern" (paragraphs 103–07). The European Economic Community's first achievement in this sphere was to create a Monetary Com-

---

27. Schoorl (1995, pp. 7–8).

28. In fact, the two influences were related. One of the European Economic Community's first achievements was the creation of the Common Agricultural Policy, which was vulnerable to disruption by exchange rate changes and hence subject to destabilization by the United States.

mittee consisting of representatives of each nation's central bank and finance ministry, plus two representatives of the European Commission. Their function was to exchange views, seek a consensus, and prepare for meetings of the Council of Ministers of Economics and Finance (ECOFIN).[29] The Committee of Central Bank Governors was created in 1964; by the time the European Monetary System was established in 1979, this committee had been meeting for fifteen years.

Still, until the 1980s there was less institutionalization than met the eye. This was reflected in the difficulty governments experienced in holding their exchange rates within the narrow bands of the Snake following the breakdown of Bretton Woods. Inspired by the report of the Werner Committee (1970), which emphasized the advantages of European monetary integration, participants in the Snake established short-term and very-short-term credit facilities to support countries with weak currencies. A European Monetary Cooperation Fund, with a board made up of governors of national central banks, was established to monitor European monetary policies, oversee the operation of credit facilities, and authorize realignments.

In practice, the European Monetary Cooperation Fund had little authority, since central bank governors were unwilling to delegate their prerogatives. For their part, the central bankers, meeting as the Committee of Governors, did little more than periodically coordinate foreign exchange market intervention.[30] In the end, there was no effective institution to monitor policies and press for adjustments. In the absence of such a mechanism, strong-currency countries could not be assured that their weak-currency counterparts would adjust. As a result, they were willing to provide only limited support.

Fiscal policy ran into similar problems. The fiscal federalism and centralization foreseen in the Werner Report, which would have helped weak-currency countries cling to the Snake, remained unrealized. Since there was no political entity in Brussels accountable to constituencies at the national level, governments refused to cede fiscal responsibility to the Community. Hence the adjustments in fiscal policies needed to hold exchange rates within the Snake were not forthcoming.

29. In addition, in the early 1960s it established a trio of committees concerned with conjunctural policy, medium-term economic policy, and budgetary policy; these were merged into a newly created Economic Policy Committee in 1974.

30. See Gros and Thygesen (1991, pp. 22–23).

These arrangements were ineffective because no consensus could be reached on policy. National officials could not agree on the appropriate response to disturbances. The idea that the mission of monetary policy should be to maintain price stability was not yet widely accepted. Policymakers had had little opportunity to experiment with expansionary monetary policy under Bretton Woods, and they failed to see how aggressive monetary expansion in an environment of unbalanced budgets could stimulate inflation rather than output and employment. Given Germany's aversion to inflation, the result was a predictable lack of cohesion.

EC member states sought to rectify these deficiencies and to restore symmetry to the operation of Europe's monetary system by creating the EMS. As envisaged by the French and German negotiators, the EMS Agreement would have replaced the moribund European Monetary Cooperation Fund with a European Monetary Fund to manage the combined foreign exchange rate reserves of the participating countries and to intervene in currency markets. Germany sought to endow the Monetary Committee with strengthened oversight powers as a way of creating a body that could hold national monetary officials accountable. One of the responsibilities of this committee was to develop a "trigger mechanism" requiring changes in domestic policies when these jeopardized currency pegs. A violation of agreed-upon indicators would force strong-currency countries such as Germany to expand and weak-currency countries such as France to contract. In return for accepting this arrangement, France secured a provision in the EMS Act of Foundation authorizing governments to draw unlimited credits from the very short-term financing facility.

The political viability of this bargain hinged on the effectiveness of oversight and of the trigger mechanism. If oversight were lax and the trigger failed to fire, Germany might be required to extend unlimited exchange rate support to its more inflation-prone EMS partners, undermining its commitment to price stability. The Bundesbank's reservations led it to obtain a letter from the finance minister, Otmar Emminger, conceding the right to opt out of its intervention obligation if the government were unable to secure an agreement with its European partners on the need to realign.[31] In return, the German government dropped its demand for a trigger mechanism.

---

31. See Emminger (1986).

Notwithstanding these compromises, the EMS of the 1980s functioned more smoothly than the Snake of the 1970s, owing to its strengthened surveillance and more generous credit lines. None of the countries that participated in the EMS saw their currencies driven out of the system, in contrast to experience under the Snake. Still, these institutions had a limited reach. In particular, they did not extend into the sphere of fiscal policies. They could not significantly shape the monetary policies of the strong-currency countries. Nor could they force countries to realign if they were reluctant to do so. This became evident in the wake of German economic and monetary unification, when countries' preferences proved to be different and the German monetary-fiscal mix placed strains on other currencies participating in the Exchange Rate Mechanism of the EMS. The European Community's institutional apparatus proved incapable of bringing about timely realignments of those currencies. It was unable to force weak-currency countries to accept budgetary retrenchment or Germany to change its policy mix. The resulting lack of policy coordination[32] culminated in the 1992–93 crisis, which drove the United Kingdom and Italy to abandon the Exchange Rate Mechanism.

Thus, although Europe has made much progress toward constructing institutions that will support the systematic and successful coordination of monetary policy, it still has some way to go. The Maastricht Treaty and the monetary union should help it move closer to this goal.

Post-EMU Europe

The European Central Bank will transform the institutions of monetary cooperation. Article 2 of the statute of the European System of Central Banks (which is made up of the ECB and the national central banks of the participating countries) identifies price stability as the ECB's primary objective. This specification illustrates both the importance of the emerging policy consensus of the 1980s and 1990s in bringing the Maastricht Treaty into being and the role of the treaty in institutionalizing that consensus.

Price stability will be sought by an Executive Board appointed when the starting date for Stage III is set. The board will have six

32. Emphasized by Buiter, Corsetti, and Pesenti (1996).

members, including the president, chosen by common accord from among the countries participating in the monetary union, acting on a recommendation of the Council of Ministers and after consulting with the European Parliament and the Governing Council of the ECB.

Executive Board members will serve long terms in office, typically eight years.[33] They will be joined on the Governing Council by the heads of the central banks of the participating countries, whose independence will be strengthened by longer terms in office. The Governing Council will make the key decisions regarding the stance of monetary policy (for example, it will set the level of interest rates), while the Executive Board will oversee the implementation of those decisions.

Insofar as exchange rate fluctuations affect price stability, responsibility for policy in this area rests with the Governing Council. At the same time, Article 109 of the Maastricht Treaty empowers the Council of Ministers, acting by qualified majority, to adopt "general orientations" for exchange rate policy with respect to currencies outside the European Union. Presumably one purpose of this provision is to leave the door open for the negotiation of Louvre-like intervention agreements. Article 109 stipulates that such orientations must not jeopardize the pursuit of price stability, but it fails to indicate who will decide whether jeopardy exists. Nor does Article 109 provide a mechanism that would make the Council's general orientations binding on the ECB.[34]

A decision to establish a system of pegged exchange rates for the industrial countries or a global system of target zones would rest with the Council of Ministers.[35] The Council must act unanimously after consulting with the ECB and attempting to reach a consensus on the compatibility of its decision with price stability. In this case the ECB must abide by the Council's decision.

As indicated earlier, efforts to coordinate monetary policies can be hampered by an inability to adjust fiscal policies. This problem could be quite severe under the institutional arrangements of Stage III. Although the monetary policies of EMU members will be run by the ECB,

---

33. Some members will serve shorter terms in office during the initial period to permit the eventual staggering of appointments.

34. See Kenen (1995), pp. 32–33.

35. On a pegged system, see Volcker (1995); on a global system, see John Williamson (1985).

fiscal policies will still be determined in national capitals. Some relief might conceivably be provided by the Mutual Surveillance Procedure of Article 103 of the Maastricht Treaty. This instructs the Council to develop guidelines for the economic policies of member states, to monitor their economic policies, and to issue recommendations should policies be inconsistent with its guidelines. However, the treaty contains no sanctions for countries that fail to respond as requested.[36]

The treaty does little to articulate a framework for monetary relations between the founding EMU members and other EU countries. Articles 44–47 and 109 provide for a General Council of the ECB, which is to include the Governing Council plus the heads of the central banks of non-EMU member states. But the responsibilities of the General Council are limited to collecting statistics and determining staffing policy.[37]

Implications for Monetary Cooperation in Europe

The Maastricht Treaty makes little mention of the EMS or of other mechanisms for coordinating monetary policy between states inside and outside EMU because European officials assumed that all EU member states would be ready to enter Stage III as soon as it began. If all countries were not ready, then the laggards were expected to join as soon as possible, anchoring exchange market expectations. On the assumption that governments would be willing and able to hold their exchange rates within narrow bands (EMS bands being $2^1/_4$ percent at the time), one of the four convergence criteria governing admission

36. The treaty also entails an excessive deficit procedure (EDP) and a pact on stability and growth (negotiated subsequently). A member state will be said to have an excessive deficit when so declared by the European Council, upon a report by the European Commission and a judgment by the Monetary Committee. The EDP is set in motion if the country's deficit and general government debt exceed 3 and 60 percent of gross domestic product, respectively, the "reference values" specified in a protocol to the treaty. While this procedure is not intended to facilitate fiscal policy coordination per se, it will encourage the exchange of information and the analysis of cross-border impacts of national policies. Whether it can be applied with the flexibility needed for the sensible coordination of fiscal policies is another matter; if rigidly enforced, it could in fact pose a barrier to coordination. See Eichengreen and von Hagen (1996). This problem will be all the more severe if the ceilings on budget deficits agreed to under the Stability Pact are strictly enforced.

37. In addition, the General Council is entitled to be informed of the decisions of the Governing Council. Only the president of the ECB and the heads of the national central banks, not the other members of the Executive Board, vote on the General Council.

was that they would do so for two years.[38] For all these reasons, then, exchange rates within the European Union were expected to be stable.

Today the situation is different. The 1992 EMS crisis drove Italy and the United Kingdom from the ERM, and the United Kingdom has made no move to rejoin. The crisis forced two new EU members, Sweden and Finland, which had previously pegged their currencies, to float, as Sweden continues to do. Fluctuation bands for the remaining participants were widened from $2^1/4$ to 15 percent, thereby increasing the scope for currency variability. Debate in Britain and Denmark made clear that these countries, which possessed opt-outs from EMU under the Maastricht Treaty, might prefer not to join, at least initially. Successive recessions underscored the difficulty of meeting the debt and deficit criteria for entry.

Under the circumstances, both insiders and outsiders ("pre-ins" in the politically correct term) will exist when Stage III begins. Mechanisms will therefore be needed to promote policy coordination between the two groups. The Mutual Surveillance Procedure mentioned earlier is one such mechanism. But it does not come with an effective enforcement technology, especially for countries that do not wish to participate in the monetary union. Although the protocol to the treaty makes two years of exchange rate stability within "normal" EMS bands an entry condition, it does not define "normal." Normal is widely taken to mean 15 percent. And even this relatively lax constraint will not bind member states that have no immediate intention of entering the monetary union.

This raises the specter of significant exchange rate fluctuations between the euro and other EU currencies, a prospect that countries such as France find alarming. The French fear competitive currency depreciation and the dumping of goods by EU member states that are not among the founding members of the monetary union. The departure of the United Kingdom and Italy from the ERM and their subsequent export-led recoveries, which arguably took place partly at French expense, resonate with France's long-standing aversion to currency fluctuations.

France, with the support of other EU governments sharing its concerns, therefore insisted that a new EMS be constructed around the

38. Certain countries that joined the ERM relatively late were allowed to operate wider 6 percent bands, but the presumption was that they would follow Italy in moving from the wide to the narrow band as soon as they were ready.

single European currency. It is to be a "hub-and-spoke system" in which the currencies of outsiders will be linked to the euro by bilateral bands (in contrast to the multilateral grid that currently links ERM currencies). Although the ECB, at its discretion, will be able to provide limited amounts of support for those currencies, each outsider will be unilaterally responsible for staying within its EMS band.[39]

However strong the argument for exchange rate bands to prevent the uncontrolled fluctuation of outsider currencies, there remains the question of viability. The history of the EMS has demonstrated the difficulty of unilaterally defending exchange rate bands in highly liquid markets. The ECB for its part will want to establish the credibility of its commitment to price stability; it will hardly be prepared to lend extensive support to currencies outside.

Thus the prospects for monetary cooperation between the EMU insiders and outsiders are unclear. The Maastricht Treaty fails to specify the institutional framework for cooperation. The 1992–93 EMS crisis undermined the policy consensus that once existed between countries such as Sweden and the United Kingdom, on the one hand, and France and Germany, on the other. These problems remain to be solved.

Implications for Transatlantic Monetary Cooperation

Without advance planning, monetary union threatens to disrupt the institutions of international monetary cooperation. In the case of Article IV consultations between the International Monetary Fund and EU states participating in the monetary union, such consultations have traditionally taken reviews of monetary policy as their responsibility; in Stage III, however, that policy will no longer be under the control of the national government in question. Nor will fiscal policy, to the extent

---

39. Insistence on a new EMS for the outsiders follows from the belief that, for its relatively open economies, the political costs of floating are prohibitively high. The more integrated European economies become, the more pronounced are the distributional consequences of intra-EU currency swings. With the perfection of the single market, EU countries that depreciate their currencies will be able to flood other member states with exports. Resistance to accepting those imports will grow as integration proceeds. Countries that violate the monetary rules of the Maastricht Treaty, the adherents will argue, are not entitled to the privileges of the single market. The implication is that uncontrolled fluctuations between the currencies of the insiders and outsiders may undermine the single market and hence be unacceptable to all concerned. We present public statements and other evidence consistent with this prospect in Eichengreen and Ghironi (1996).

that the latter is influenced by the Mutual Surveillance and Excessive Deficit Procedures of the European Union. Little thought has yet been given to these implications of EMU for the coordinating role of the IMF.

The situation is much the same for G-7 summits. Since 1977 it has been standard practice for the president of the European Commission to attend these summits, along with the leader of the country holding the presidency of the Council of Ministers.[40] In the late 1970s meetings of the Council were always timed to occur shortly before the summit in an effort to define a common EC position and maximize the coherence of bargaining positions. In recent years, however, coordination between EC and national representatives has been loose at best.

But neither the president of the European Commission nor the finance minister of the country holding the presidency of the Council can speak for the European Central Bank, which will control the levers of monetary policy for the euro zone. The ECB cannot speak for Britain if it remains outside the monetary union. It will, however, represent Austria, Ireland, Spain, Portugal, Finland, and the Benelux countries, which are not members of the G-7 (but are among the founding members of the monetary union).

The president of the Commission is an appropriate spokesman for EU fiscal authorities to the extent that the stance of fiscal policy in member states is shaped by the Council, the Commission, and the Monetary Committee's administration of the Excessive Deficit and Mutual Surveillance Procedures. But countries with surpluses will still control their own fiscal policies; although in principle the Mutual Surveillance Procedure applies to them as well, in practice they are likely to retain considerable autonomy. In any case, it is far from clear that the Excessive Deficit and Mutual Surveillance Procedures will be strictly enforceable. (Note that the Mutual Surveillance Procedure also applied in Stage II, in which countries displayed little willingness to delegate responsibility for fiscal policies to the Council of Ministers.) Thus the existence of overlapping monetary and fiscal competencies suggests that complications will increase, not decrease. It is unlikely, therefore, that G-7 summits of finance ministers and central bankers can be telescoped into a G-3 format.[41]

---

40. The Commission has participated in a discussion of all questions arising at the summit, not just those directly involving the European Community. See Putnam and Bayne (1987).

41. This is a reference to Bergsten and Henning (1996), who argue the opposite.

Moreover, the attempt to reach Louvre-style agreements may founder on the inability of the Council and ECB to agree among themselves. Article 109 of the Maastricht Treaty empowers the Council to adopt general orientations for exchange rate policy in relation to non-EU currencies, a clause that is meant to permit the negotiation of agreements regarding intervention in foreign exchange markets. But Article 109 does not bind the ECB to accept and to act upon the Council's general orientations. The ECB may opt out of such orientations if they conflict with price stability.[42]

In fact, there is unlikely to be a strong consensus in favor of monetary cooperation in the early phases of Stage III. With the creation of a European economic and monetary union, Europe will become more of a large, relatively closed economy, like the United States.[43] The bulk of member states' commercial and financial transactions already take place with other member states. Theories suggesting a further expansion of transactions within the integrated economic zone imply that this will be even more true in the future. Exchange rate fluctuations in relation to the rest of the world will then become less disruptive. According to the theory of optimum currency areas, such a relatively large, closed economy will be inclined to float its currency.[44] If so, the United States will find it harder to enlist the ECB and Europe's governments in Louvre-style operations. Similarly, Europe will respond less eagerly to any U.S. initiative to create a system of exchange rate pegs or target zones.

In its early years the ECB will be reluctant to commit itself to concerted foreign exchange market intervention. Its overriding commitment will be to price stability. Evincing excessive interest in other

42. According to Kenen (1995, p. 32), it is widely agreed that the ECB will decide this for itself, although this is not specified in the treaty. The Council or even the European Parliament, to which the president and Executive Board of the ECB may be called to testify, might be able to exercise the political leverage needed to get the ECB to accept its general orientations. The heat thrown off by the television lights of parliamentary hearing rooms may make it uncomfortable for the ECB to resist. On the other hand, the most powerful lever normally available to national parliaments seeking to influence their independent central banks is the threat to circumscribe their statutory independence. This sanction is not available to the European Parliament, since the ECB statute is part of an international treaty that can be modified only with the unanimous consent of the signatory countries.

43. Initially, we adopt a long-run perspective compatible with the assumption that all EU member states participate in the monetary union. We then attempt to draw out some of the implications of two-speed monetary union for transatlantic relations.

44. Empirical evidence to this effect is provided in Bayoumi and Eichengreen (1996).

targets, including the exchange rate, may be seen as calling that commitment into doubt. The Governing Board will be inclined to follow a stringent interpretation of Article 109, rejecting the Council's general orientations when they seem incompatible with price stability. This makes monetary policy coordination along the lines of the Plaza and the Louvre less likely in the initial years of Stage III.

This point applies with even greater force to schemes for pegged exchange rates or G-7 target zones. The unanimous consent of the Council of Ministers needed before the ECB can enter into such an arrangement is a high hurdle.[45] Although the ECB would then be bound by the Council's decision, the threat that its board might object in a way that damaged the Council's reputation for financial probity, not to mention the viability of the exchange rate agreement, would give the ECB at least potential veto power (akin to the Bundesbank's sway over the German chancellor at certain junctures). And the aforementioned argument suggests that it would be inclined to exercise that power in the early years of Stage III.[46]

A multispeed EMU would complicate matters further. Fluctuations in the foreign exchange value of the dollar have long strained the EMS.[47] If EMU insiders and outsiders establish a new EMS designed to limit the movement of other EU currencies against the euro and the European Central Bank is responsible for its operation, then the ECB will also acquire an interest in stabilizing the dollar exchange rate and may therefore be more favorably inclined to agree to wider exchange rate stabilization. Working in the other direction are the limited reserves of the ECB and its concern with the inflationary effects of intervention. Intervention to limit the dollar's decline, intended to insulate the weak EMS currencies, will then discourage direct intervention on behalf of those currencies. Knowledge of this tradeoff may dim the ECB's enthusiasm for a wider agreement.

45. Henning (1996) therefore recommends revising Article 109 to permit the Council to endorse such an arrangement by a simple or qualified majority vote.

46. How such a conflict would play out is unclear. In 1978–79, when the Bundesbank objected to the EMS negotiation, it obtained the Emminger letter. But in 1990–91, when it objected to immediate German monetary unification at a conversion rate of one to one, it was unable to hold the line. In any case, it is unlikely that the Council will be willing to force the issue until confidence in the ECB is well established.

47. Official analyses (Commission of the European Communities, 1993; Committee of Governors of the Central Banks, 1993) assign them a place of prominence in explaining the 1992–93 crisis, for example.

With the onset of Stage III, other interest groups will conceivably gain more say over transatlantic monetary cooperation. Industrial groups in France, for example, which have traditionally complained about the disruptive effects of currency swings on profitability, will shift their attention from the deutsche mark to the dollar and the yen. (There has already been some evidence of this, as in 1996, when the franc–deutsche mark rate remained relatively stable, but fluctuations in the dollar and the yen aggravated the difficulties of the French economy, eliciting complaints about U.S. and Japanese policy in the French press.) Moreover, in the early years of Stage III the dollar and yen exchange rates will be obvious indicators of the ECB's success in carrying out its mandate to pursue price stability. By contrast, the information content of the new price index for the euro zone will not yet be clear. Whether the euro rises or falls against the dollar will be a more obvious measure of success. Although the ECB may be reluctant to formally stabilize the euro against the dollar and the yen, it may favor informal initiatives designed to deliver that result.

Strengthening the Framework for International Monetary Cooperation

Regrettably, the scope for strengthening transatlantic monetary cooperation remains even more limited. It seems unlikely that the G-7 countries, or even the United States and Japan alone, will be able to agree on a durable system of exchange rate target zones as the centerpiece of rejuvenated G-7 cooperation.[48] Also unrealistic is the idea that the United States could demand a revision of Article 109 of the Maastricht Treaty to remove unanimity within the European Council as a precondition for the construction of any new global exchange rate regime. The same is true of proposals to revise the complicated procedure by which the ECB might agree to participate in a future Louvre-style accord. This is not to deny that it would be helpful for the Council and the ECB and their American counterparts to clarify the conditions under which they might contemplate such operations. The G-7 as presently constituted is not an ideal venue for this process, since the president of the European Commission, who participates in

48. For a detailed argument as to why such a system is unlikely to be feasible, see Eichengreen (1994). In contrast, Bergsten and Henning (1996) do see such a system in the offing.

those meetings, speaks only indirectly for the Council. This is another argument for coordinating Council meetings with G-7 summits. It supports the practice of including both the president of the Commission and the finance minister of the country currently holding the presidency of the Council.

Article IV consultations with individual EU member states will have to be supplemented with Article IV consultations with the European Union itself, insofar as the institutions of the European Union will determine the monetary policy of EMU participants and influence, through the Excessive Deficit and Mutual Surveillance Procedures, the fiscal policies of all fifteen member states. Consultations with the EU member states participating in EMU should not be abolished; the latter will still be able to draw on their quotas, and it is with the individual member states that the Fund will presumably continue to conclude stand-by agreements. But these parallel consultations are a potential source of confusion: for example, both the Fund and the European Union might make loans to member states in fiscal and financial difficulty but lay down conflicting conditions. It would be as if the Fund held Article IV consultations not just with the U.S. government but with each of the country's fifty states. This points to the importance of having the Fund coordinate with the European Union.

In principle, EMU should be an occasion for restructuring EU representation at the Fund. Because EMU members will no longer experience payments problems induced by the exchange rate in dealings with one another, any more than one Federal Reserve district can have an unsustainable balance of payments with another, there is an argument for netting out intra-EMU trade and financial flows when calculating Fund quotas. This would reduce the voting power of the EMU member states.[49] It would provide an opportunity to meet Japan's long-standing demand for a quota increase and to take into account the rise of new trading powers. Doing so would enhance the legitimacy of the Fund, which is viewed elsewhere in the world as

49. At present, the votes of France, Germany, Austria, Ireland, and the Benelux countries nearly match those of the United States. Still, it is hard to imagine the EMU members voting as a bloc at the IMF, given the fact that members of the Executive Board represent groups of countries, and prospective EMU states are grouped together with non-EU members in the various constituencies. To take the point to its logical extreme, this is an argument for reconfiguring constituencies so that all EMU states belong to a single constituency.

unfairly dominated by North Atlantic interests. These changes in global economic relations should be acknowledged if the IMF is to retain the legitimacy required of a major player in the policy coordination process.[50]

There is reason to think that the focus of monetary cooperation in coming years will shift to containing financial crises in countries such as Mexico, Thailand, and South Korea.[51] It may be necessary to provide international-lender-of-last-resort assistance or to help restructure such countries' external debts. The Mexican crisis illustrates both the need for such measures and the obstacles to coordination. The response mounted by the industrial countries lacked an institutional mechanism through which the requisite financial resources could be assembled and deployed, and no consensus was reached on the form such intervention should take. The timing and severity of the crisis came as a surprise to the international policy community, whose early warning system was found wanting. Meeting it required unprecedented levels of finance, forcing the United States and other G-10 governments to supplement IMF resources in an ad hoc fashion.[52] IMF procedures did not allow the Executive Board to respond with the speed required. Normal consensus building had to be short-circuited, and this caused some recrimination, which led certain European governments to abstain on the final vote on the Mexican loan.

Some progress has now been made toward rectifying these deficiencies. The IMF has taken steps to speed the dissemination of data by its members and to strengthen early warning systems. It has established a data dissemination standard to be met by its members and a special standard to be met by actual or prospective borrowers on international capital markets. It has established an emergency financing mechanism to speed the disbursal of funds.

These new procedures were put to their first test in the Asian currency crisis of 1997. The Fund acted faster, and with less angst, than

50. A stumbling block for advocates of quota revision is the fact that monetary union is a moving target. The number of participants will continue to change as current EU members are progressively admitted and as the European Union expands to the east. This militates against a change in quotas when EMU arrives. It also makes it a more complex task for the Fund to treat the monetary union as a unit for Article IV consultation purposes.

51. This argument is further developed in Eichengreen (1997).

52. In the U.S. case, through the Clinton administration's resort to the Exchange Stabilization Fund.

three years before. Japan, for obvious reasons, played a more prominent role in marshaling support. It was not necessary to determine whether the Thai crisis threatened to destabilize the international monetary system and therefore qualified for support from the GAB because much of the $16 billion package was provided by Japan (whose banks had a considerable stake in Thai financial stability), China (which wished to assert its interest in events in the region), and other Asian countries that had just recently taken initiatives to strengthen central bank cooperation and wished to demonstrate their resolve. The same was true of the response to Korea's crisis: the IMF and G-10 governments responded quickly with a financial package of unprecedented size.

But more remains to be done to prepare the international community to deal with future financial crises.[53] Ever-growing rescue packages are neither feasible nor desirable; sometimes countries should simply write down and restructure no longer viable debts, in which case the problem becomes one of cleaning up after the fact. Creating an institutionalized venue for negotiations between bondholders' representatives and the governments of countries forced to suspend service payments on their sovereign debts will be effective only if governments do their part by sanctioning the establishment of standing bondholders' committees. The proposal that the IMF consider extending credit before a country has cleared away its arrears, in order to provide countries with working capital to support their financial systems and economies while restructuring is still under way, does not yet command a critical mass of support among Fund members. And, as mentioned earlier, access by noncontributors to the GAB is limited to countries whose difficulties pose a threat to the international monetary and financial system, which some European officials did not grant in the case of the Mexican crisis and might not have granted in the case of the Thai crisis in 1997. For a country without the strategic and economic importance of a Mexico or a Korea, contributions from the leading national governments will be more difficult to assemble. Instead it will be necessary to clarify and liberalize the terms of access to the GAB. If for political reasons this is not possible, there is a case for an IMF quota increase to provide the requisite resources by other means.

53. Here we summarize the conclusions of Eichengreen and Portes (1996).

Conclusion

Cultivating international monetary cooperation is a slow, laborious, and incremental process that requires an elaborate institutional framework and deep policy consensus. International monetary cooperation between Europe, the United States, and Japan remains sporadic at best. And with the introduction of the euro and the European Central Bank, even today's relatively limited arrangements may be disrupted. This chapter has suggested some modest steps for encouraging institution building and consensus formation within Europe, across the Atlantic, and among the community of nations generally.

The European perspective has one additional implication. Monetary cooperation is extensive in Europe because it is linked to other issue areas. The European Monetary System, for example, is linked to the common agricultural policy and the internal market, both of which can be disrupted by exchange rate fluctuations, while monetary union is linked both to the internal market and to Germany's agenda of political integration. More extensive U.S.-European cooperation on other issues, such as transatlantic free trade, would similarly work to create comparable linkages across the Atlantic and thereby encourage monetary cooperation.

Chapter 5

European Migration Policies in American Perspective

Riccardo Faini

M igration is one of the most divisive issues in industrial societies, particularly in Europe. It inspires passions and fears. Those opposing immigration are afraid that it will stir social tensions, blur European identities, and exacerbate Europe's unemployment and poverty problems. Those who advocate a less restrictive approach see considerable benefit in a multiracial and multicultural society, both from a demographic and economic point of view. Most people would agree, however, that unrestricted migration is not a viable policy option.

Europe's attitude toward migration has changed markedly since the years between 1955 and 1974, when it was actively promoted by the governments of receiving countries. Because of widespread labor shortages—the unemployment rate in Germany had fallen to less than 1 percent in 1961–66—migration was considered a means of achieving sustained and rapid growth in those countries. As a result, at least 10.5 million people crossed European borders during that period, moving mainly from Southern to Northern Europe. The turnaround came after 1974, when, in the aftermath of the first oil shock, economic growth slowed and unemployment soared to unprecedented levels. As a result, traditionally receiving countries adopted a very restrictive stance toward migration policy that proved to be far from a temporary change. Contrary to expectations, Europe's economic slump and its unemployment persisted, as the jobless rate rose steadily from 1974 until 1987. Although the economic recovery after 1987 brought a sizable reduction in the unemployment rate, these gains were reversed after 1991.

It seems that any economic recoveries since 1974 have only been able to slow down or at best temporarily reverse the upward trend in Europe's unemployment. Not surprisingly, immigration policy has remained restrictive throughout this period. But widespread unemployment at home was only one of the factors working against a resumption of migration. Potential migrants are mostly unskilled laborers, and this became a disadvantage in the 1980s: the pattern of technological progress was biased against unskilled workers, and the growing competition from emerging developing countries, which had brought increasing pressure on labor-intensive sectors using unskilled workers, shifted the demand for labor away from less educated workers. Whereas in the 1950s and 1960s the migrants were in great demand, this was no longer the case in the 1980s.

The more hostile attitude toward migration was also related to a growth in social tensions, which were not as prevalent during the 1950s and 1960s, even during massive migration flows. For the most part, migration was temporary then, either because of an explicit policy choice, as in Switzerland, or because of immigrants' own decisions. After 1974 the situation changed. Gross immigration declined markedly, but so did return migration. An increasing proportion of migrants no longer wanted to return home, but rather leaned toward settling in the host country for a longer period of time. Paradoxically, this fall in the propensity to return may well be related to the more restrictive stance in migration policy after 1974. Migrants knew that if they returned home, they would have much more difficulty reentering the host country. Furthermore, the very nature of migration flows had changed. Family reunification became a larger component of total population flows. New migrants were now coming to stay. Old migrants were less willing to return. The integration of migrants had thus become a central issue in the design of migration policies. Yet it was soon realized that assimilation policies could be truly effective only in the medium and long run. In the short run, integration faces severe hurdles, as can be seen in the disproportionate burden of unemployment on the shoulders of foreigners, and is often accompanied by rising social tensions among both natives and migrants.

The new pattern of migration during the 1970s and 1980s drew a twofold policy response from the receiving countries.[1] First, they moved to control immigration and, whenever possible, encourage

1. Collinson (1993).

returns (schemes to encourage return migration were launched in France and Germany, but they met with limited success). Second, they made it a policy imperative to integrate existing migrants into Europe's societies in order to prevent further social tension. These assimilation policies ranged from that of the Netherlands, which called on citizens to respect the cultural and linguistic traditions of immigrants, to that of France, which encouraged immigrants to adopt French culture and values.

Despite difficulties, this two-pronged policy approach seemed to work well enough, at least until the political upheaval in Eastern Europe at the end of the 1980s: in 1989 alone, approximately 1,150 thousand migrants moved to Germany. The flow continued in the following years. At the same time, Europe's southern frontier was at risk. Explosive demographic trends together with continuing economic stagnation in much of the developing world, particularly in Africa, made massive, and largely undesired, migrations a distinct possibility. Was Europe under siege? Was the old policy inadequate to cope with the new situation? These are some of the questions examined in this chapter.

European Migrations

Migration is an enduring feature of European economic history. In the nineteenth century, migrants left Europe in large numbers in search of better living and working conditions. Most of them went overseas, mainly to the Americas. Yet, migration was also sustained within Europe. Between 1890 and 1913, for instance, 6.6 million Italians migrated to the United States or to Latin America, while 4.9 million went to European destinations.[2] Migration came to a standstill in the interwar period, mainly because of restrictive U.S. immigration policies and the effects of the Great Depression. Population flows resumed on a massive scale after World War II, initially because of the war itself: 12 million Germans were forced to leave Eastern Europe by 1950.[3] But from that time on, Northern Europeans no longer felt compelled to emigrate. Rapid and sustained growth in Northern Europe soon led to widespread labor shortages, prompting governments there to actively recruit foreign workers, particularly

2. Ferenczi and Willcox (1931).
3. Zimmermann (1995a).

from Southern Europe. From 1955 to 1973, approximately 10.5 million migrants crossed European borders, mainly from Southern to Northern Europe.[4] A large number also came from North Africa and Turkey.

The period of restricted migration began in 1974, in the wake of the first oil shock. Rising unemployment at home and falling demand for migrant labor led governments in the receiving countries to restrict new immigration. But these efforts were not successful, mainly because of the decline in return migration and the rise in family reunification. For Germany, for instance, the share of working migrants in total migration fluctuated around 10 percent during the 1980s. Even after the massive migration inflows after 1989, nonworking migrants still represented more than 70 percent of total migration. Similarly, the share of nonworking migrants in France has been consistently larger than 70 percent since 1983. Often, though, family migration simply masked worker migration, as family members were keen to take jobs in the host country. Moreover, political immigration was on the rise during the 1980s, again often as a way of circumventing restrictive admission policies. Equally important, it is believed that the size of illegal migration increased markedly during this decade.

The upheaval in Eastern Europe after 1989 opened a new era in the history of European migration. For several decades, economic links between Eastern and Western Europe had been artificially severed. During the cold war, the West was eager to criticize socialist governments for imposing tight restrictions on the freedom of people to move, particularly to the West. When the Iron Curtain was raised, however, governments in the West quickly imposed stringent migration controls of their own for fear of massive immigration flows. Population flows were indeed large after 1989, particularly to Germany. Whereas gross migration had averaged 400,000 between 1984 and 1987, the number that moved to Germany in 1989 totaled 770,800, and the figure rose to 920,500 in 1991 and to 1.21 million in 1992. If ethnic Germans were included (they are not counted as migrants in German statistics), the figure for 1989 would have soared to 1.15 million. Other countries in Europe also experienced a sudden increase in immigration. In the Netherlands the stock of foreign population in-

4. Razin and Sadka (1995).

FIGURE 5-1. *Migration Rates from Southen Europe, 1961–88*

Per thousand

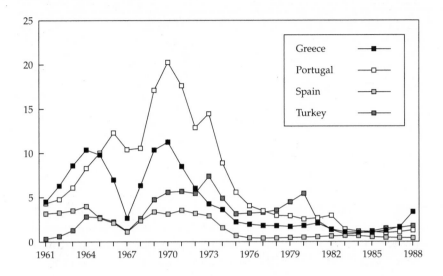

creased by almost 40 percent, from an average of 554,000 in the period 1983–85 to 757,000 during 1991–93.

An equally dramatic change had in the meantime taken place in Southern Europe. In the 1950s and 1960s countries such as Greece, Italy, Spain, and Portugal had been a steady source of migrant labor for Northern Europe. Migration from Southern Europe reached a peak around 1971 (figure 5-1) but then fell sharply after the first oil shock. When the economic recovery was well under way in Northern Europe, migrations from the south did not resume. On the contrary, most Southern European countries turned into immigration countries. As table 5-1 shows, foreign residents almost doubled between 1980 and 1988 in Italy, Spain, and Portugal. This was indeed a striking historical shift. The countries of Southern Europe were no longer exporting labor to Northern Europe and had become themselves the destination for emigratory flows, mainly from North Africa.

Thus at the beginning of the 1990s two regions, Eastern Europe and North Africa, represented the main potential sources of migration to Europe. With the dissolution of socialism, Eastern Europeans were no longer forcibly tied to their home country but could leave for Western

TABLE 5-1. *Foreign Residents in Southern Europe, 1980–93*

Thousands

Year	Italy	Spain	Portugal
1980	298.7	181.5	58.1
1982	358.9	200.9	68.2
1984	403.9	226.5	89.6
1986	450.2	293.2	86.9
1988	645.4	360	95
1990	781.1	278.8	n.a.
1993	987.4	430.4	131.6

Source: SOPEMI (1995).
n.a. Not available.

Europe in droves. At the same time, economic and demographic factors combined to increase the migration potential in North Africa, a region that had already been the source of large population flows toward Europe some years earlier. The appearance of new destinations in Southern Europe also made Europe as a whole more attractive to potential migrants. The preferred destination of migrants from Eastern Europe was Germany, while migrants from North Africa made their way toward the northern shore of the Mediterranean, to France, Italy, and Spain.

How Large Is the "Migration Threat"?

The "nightmare" scenario for European immigration has several components. First, if the formerly planned economies of Central and Eastern Europe failed to achieve a successful and peaceful transition to the market system, the resulting social and economic disruption in those countries would prompt individuals to seek better and safer living conditions abroad. Ethnic conflicts and outright wars would boost the flow of refugees toward Western Europe. Second, economic stagnation and a growing debt burden in the developing world would force an increasing share of this rapidly growing population to make its way into the prosperous economies of Europe. This time the migration response could be stronger than in the past, in that falling transport and communication costs make it easier for populations in developing countries to learn about opportunities in the industrial world and to bear the migration costs.

Even if the nightmare scenario does not materialize, policymakers in Europe will remain concerned about the migration threat that economic and political instability in Europe's poorer neighbors may pose. In the short run, an economic slowdown in either Eastern Europe or in North Africa could put increasing migration pressure on Western Europe's porous borders. In the long run, demographic imbalances may play an even larger role in fostering massive migration. Describing potential population flows as a migration threat clearly obscures the undisputable benefits that immigration brings to the receiving country, as explained in the next section.

The extent of the migration threat can be assessed in part by examining the factors that cause people to move across international borders. The choice to migrate can be seen as the outcome of a cost-benefit calculation. Economics (and common sense) indicate that large migration flows can be triggered by a combination of geographical proximity, wide economic disparities, and demographic imbalances. The first factor, geographical proximity, is associated with lower migration costs. Similarly, substantial economic disparities raise the economic benefits of migration. Demographic factors also affect the cost-benefit calculus, since not everybody in the sending country's population will be willing to migrate. Migration is indeed costly, both in economic and psychological terms, even if it brings tangible benefits, mostly in the form of higher future earnings. The obvious implication is that elderly people are less likely to migrate: because their life expectancy is shorter than that of other members of the population, future benefits are unlikely to outweigh immediate costs in their case. From the point of view of economic incentives, then, the potential for migration is likely to rise with the share of youth in the sending country population. In short, both economic and demographic factors determine the extent of the migration threat.

The role of economic factors can be seen in income differentials between representative pairs of sending and receiving countries: the areas chosen for the purposes of comparison in this discussion are Central Europe (Poland and Hungary) and Germany; North Africa (Tunisia and Morocco) and France; and Mexico and the United States (figure 5-2). Here, income differentials are measured by real income at international prices (that is, prices corrected for purchasing power parity). The first point to note is that the economic incentive to

FIGURE 5-2. *Differentials in Purchasing Power Parity Income, 1990*

Percent

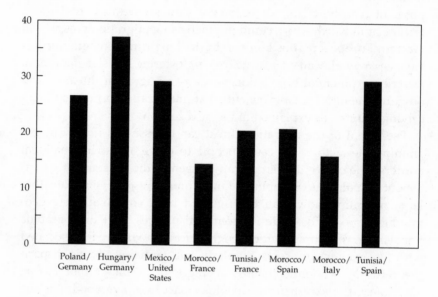

migrate between North Africa and Europe is much greater than that between Eastern and Western Europe. Seen in that light, the true migration threat to Europe does not seem to come from Eastern Europe. Second, the income differential between North Africa and Europe is substantially greater than that between Mexico and the United States. This would indicate that policymakers in Europe have more reason than those in the United States to be concerned about economic developments in their poorer neighbors in the South.

Furthermore, the incentive to migrate between North Africa and Europe may be larger than that between Southern and Northern Europe during the 1960s, namely at a time when Southern European workers were migrating on a massive scale. As figure 5-3 shows, in 1960 income per capita in Greece and Portugal barely reached 30 percent of Germany's income. A comparison of figures 5-2 and 5-3 indicates that the income gap between Southern and Northern Europe in the 1960s was smaller than the present differential between North Africa and the main European destinations. Figure 5-3 also shows that the incentive to migrate from Southern to Northern Europe (as measured by the income gap between Greece and

FIGURE 5-3. *Evolution of the Income Gap, 1960–90*

Percent

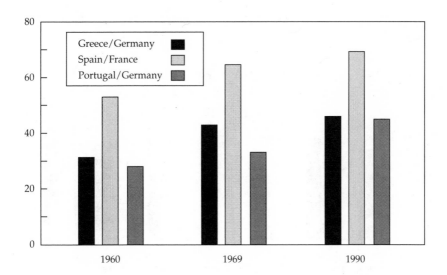

Germany, Portugal and Germany, and Spain and France) has declined substantially.

Admittedly, comparisons of income per capita can paint a somewhat misleading picture, in that migrants do not bring capital with them and are entitled only to the returns to labor. A more apt comparison would be based on wages, but such data are difficult to compile. This discussion is based on data from the International Labor Office. Wide wage gaps between receiving and sending countries can also be seen in figure 5-4. In this case, the gap is particularly marked for Poland (with respect to Germany) and for Morocco (relative to France). It is lowest for Mexico (in relation to the United States). Moreover, Poland and Mexico appear to move some way toward closing the wage gap with respect to their richer neighbor, whereas the differential between Morocco with respect to France and Spain does not change much. Again, this pattern seems to suggest that the incentive to migrate is substantially stronger between North Africa and Europe than between the United States and Mexico, or between Eastern and Western Europe.

This conclusion is further strengthened by the demographic situa-

FIGURE 5-4. *The Wage Gap, 1990 and 1993*

Percent

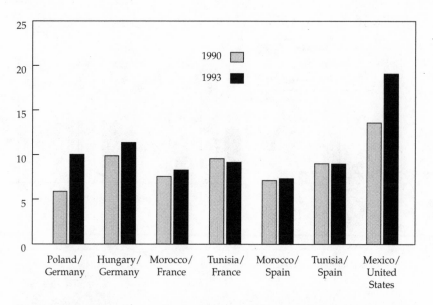

tion and prospects in sending and receiving areas. Figures 5-5 and 5-6 depict the demographic structure in Europe, the United States, Mexico, and North Africa. They show both the estimated structure in 1990 and the projected structure in 2025, by which time the age pyramid shrinks completely in Europe (and is replaced by a T-shaped structure). The same pattern appears in a milder form in the United States. Conversely, in the sending regions, the age composition in North Africa still presents a strong pyramidal structure in 2025, whereas in Mexico it becomes harder to detect. These changes in population structure are associated with a wide variation in the rates of population growth. Total population is projected to increase by 100 percent in North Africa, 65 percent in Mexico, 11.6 percent in Europe (inclusive of the former Soviet Union), and 18 percent in the United States. Particularly significant are the percentage and level of increase among those between fifteen and twenty-four years of age (table 5-2), the group of greatest interest since it includes a disproportionate share of highly mobile people. Both the share and the absolute number of this group decline markedly in Western Europe. Eastern Europe does not seem to be able to fill the gap, as the share of those

FIGURE 5-5. *Age Structure, 1990 and 2025*

Percent of Total Population

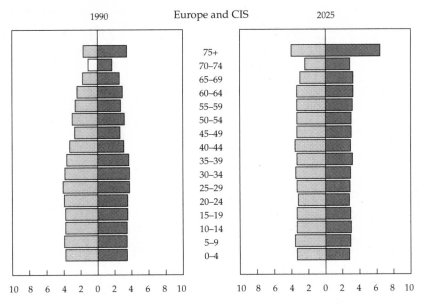

Europe and CIS

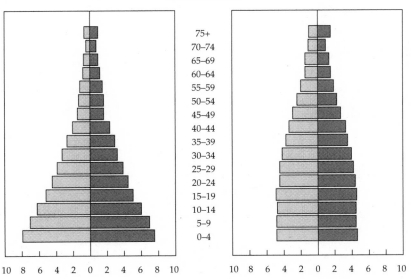

Northern Africa

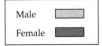

FIGURE 5-6. *Age Structure, 1990 and 2025*

Percent of Total Population

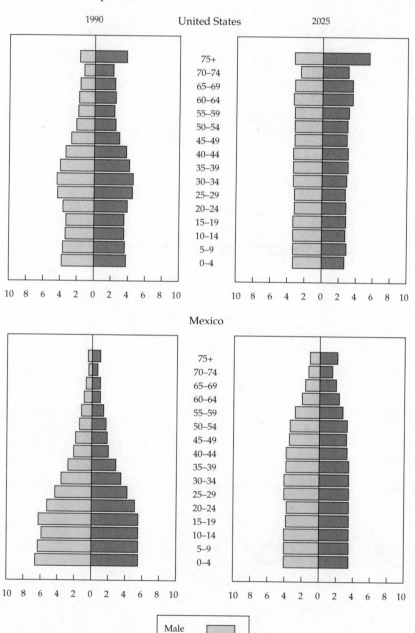

TABLE 5-2. *Population Projections, 1990–2025*

Percentage and levels of the cohort fifteen to twenty-four years old[a]

Region	1990	2000	2010	2025
Western Europe				
Percent	14.6	12.0	12.1	11.5
Level	25,690	21,974	22,665	21,700
Eastern Europe				
Percent	14.6	15.6	13.2	14.2
Level	14,102	15,483	13,635	15,219
North Africa				
Percent	19.5	20.1	19.3	18.3
Level	27,394	35,958	42,700	51,308
United States				
Percent	14.8	13.4	13.8	12.5
Level	36,996	36,893	40,860	40,251
Mexico				
Percent	22.3	19.5	18.6	15.7
Level	18,840	19,998	22,033	21,585

Source: *World Population Prospects,* United Nations (1993).
a. Levels in thousands of units.

fourteen to twenty-four years old declines somewhat, whereas the aggregate figure in 2025 is not much different from that in 1990. The picture changes dramatically in North Africa. The population share of the cohort fourteen to twenty-four years old is much higher than in Europe, although it starts declining quite rapidly after the year 2000. This, however, does not prevent the sheer number from increasing at a staggering rate, from 27 million in 1990 to a projected level of 51 million in 2025. A comparison with the United States and Mexico is again quite instructive. The projections indicate that the United States should experience an absolute increase in the cohort aged fifteen to twenty-four, whereas the rise in Mexico for the same group is substantially less marked than in North Africa.

Overall, it appears that any migration threat to Europe will come from North Africa, not from Eastern Europe. Both economic and demographic factors indicate that the pressure to migrate is substantially larger on the southern shore of the Mediterranean than on the eastern side of the former Iron Curtain. A comparison with the U.S.-Mexico situation suggests that both pull factors (that is, the wage gap with respect to the receiving country) and push factors (rapid demographic growth in the sending country) are somewhat stronger in encouraging migration from North Africa to Europe than from Mexico to the United States.

Some caution should be exercised in interpreting these results, however. Migration does not occur simply because of wage or demographic differences. Migration may be low even in the face of large earnings differentials if migrants do not believe that they have a reasonable chance of finding a job in the host country. In this respect, the U.S. economy has performed much better than the European economies. First, unemployment is substantially lower in the United States than in Europe: 6 percent against 11.5 percent. Second, employment growth has been quite impressive in the United States, averaging 1.54 percent a year over the period 1982–94. In contrast, employment growth in Europe has been almost imperceptible, amounting to only 0.15 percent over the same period. Slow employment growth and high unemployment rates could deter many would-be migrants from moving to Europe, whereas a more buoyant labor market situation may still attract migrants to the United States. Europe's labor market situation may also work toward a reduction in the demand for migrant labor. For one thing, unemployment in Europe is disproportionately concentrated among unskilled workers. For another, the pattern of technological progress should, because of its unskilled labor-saving nature, reduce the demand for the very kind of labor that is overrepresented among migrants. Some analysts have indeed concluded that these factors combine to virtually eliminate the need for further (unskilled) migration to Europe.

Yet one should not rush to conclude that Europe does not need migrants or that migrants are unwilling to move to Europe because of the lack of employment opportunities. In fact, the demand for migrant labor is still very strong, particularly in the underground economy and for those jobs that natives are not always willing to take. Furthermore, the rise of new destinations in southern Europe (with a thriving informal sector) adds to the attractiveness of migrating to Europe. In addition, wage differences are large enough to make migration profitable, even if migrants do not hold a regular job. Moroccans are still crossing the Straits of Gibraltar in makeshift boats.

Albanian shipowners are still prospering by carrying illegal migrants to the shores of Italy. Paradoxically, the high unemployment regions of southern Italy and southern Spain are hosting an increasingly large number of mostly illegal migrants. Despite high unemployment, migrants are thus still likely to come to Europe or at least are still likely to try to elude the controls that policymakers are busily establishing along Europe's external borders. Although high unemployment rates will certainly prompt policymakers in Europe to attempt to stem migrations, they are unlikely to deter would-be migrants from trying their chance in the formal and the informal sectors in the receiving countries.

The Impact of Migration on the Receiving Country

The inflow of foreign workers can affect several aspects of the domestic economy, most notably the labor market. Suppose that migration brings mostly unskilled workers. For given demand, this should lead to a fall in the unskilled wage. If wages are rigid downward, say, because of labor market regulations or union pressure, the increase in supply will result in a rise of unemployment. At the same time, unskilled migration may boost the demand for skilled workers if skilled and unskilled workers are complementary in production. One would then expect unskilled migration also to be associated with a rise in both the employment and wages of skilled labor.

Whereas theoretical predictions are quite easy to make, it is more difficult to arrive at a quantitative assessment of the impact of migration on the labor market. Typically, analysts try to establish a correlation between the share of foreign labor and other labor market characteristics such as wages and unemployment. This is done either on a geographical basis (by considering, say, European regions or standard metropolitan areas in the United States) or on a sectoral basis. The results do not seem to indicate a significant impact of migration on either wages or unemployment:[5] regions (or sectors) with a high share of foreign labor do not seem to pay lower wages or experience higher unemployment rates. However, these findings are vitiated by methodological problems. First, migrants are likely to be attracted to regions that pay above-average wages or have below-average

5. Friedberg and Hunt (1995).

unemployment rates. Therefore it is not surprising to find that regions with a large share of foreign workers do not pay lower wages and do not exhibit higher unemployment. Second, if immigration depresses wages or increases unemployment, natives may respond by moving to other regions, until wages and unemployment rates are equalized across regions. Again, migration appears to have no significant impact on the labor market condition of a given geographical area. The latter problem seems less relevant for Europe, where geographical mobility among natives is known to be quite low.[6]

   More sophisticated studies try to control for these biases either by using more appropriate econometric techniques or by focusing on event studies (such as the Mariel boatlift to Miami or the immigration of Algerian expatriates to France in 1962). They then find a statistically significant but quantitatively small effect of migration. According to one such survey, based for the most part on data from the United States, "Economic theory is equivocal, and empirical estimates in a variety of settings and using a variety of approaches have shown that the effect of immigration on the labor market outcomes of natives is small."[7]

   Somewhat surprisingly, empirical evidence on the impact of migration in Europe is quite limited. Most studies refer to Germany and Austria, two countries that have experienced a sizable increase in migration, particularly from Eastern Europe. On the whole, the evidence for Europe does not suggest a substantial impact of foreign workers on the employment of natives. A significant but quantitatively small effect of immigration on unemployment has been reported for the 1970s.[8] The results change in the 1980s: in that decade, immigration no longer had a significant impact on unemployment.[9] The same conclusion has been reached by relying on a two-stage approach, that is, by first regressing the probability of individual unemployment on individual characteristics and regional dummies and then looking at the relationship between regional dummies and regional immigration shares.[10] Results from Austria also support the view of a negligible effect of immigration on unemployment: there,

6. Eichengreen (1992); Faini (1996).
7. Friedberg and Hunt (1995).
8. Winkelman and Zimmermann (1993).
9. Muhleisen and Zimmermann (1994).
10. Hatzius (1994).

immigration does not affect the unemployment probability of young native or of blue-collar workers, but it does have a positive impact on unemployment duration.[11]

The surprisingly small employment effect of immigration suggests a few noteworthy implications. To begin with, the wage impact of foreign workers is not negligible. Indeed, it has been shown that, following a 1 percent increase in the share of foreign labor, the wage of white-collar workers will rise by 3.4 percent, but the wage of blue-collar workers will fall by 5.9 percent.[12] This is consistent with the view that migrants are mostly unskilled, whereas blue- and white-collar workers are complementary in production. These results indicate that, contrary to conventional wisdom, German wages respond flexibly to a labor market shock such as an inflow of foreign workers. In turn, wage flexibility may arise to the extent that immigration erodes institutional constraints, such as union power and labor market regulations, which have kept European wages too high and represent a significant cause of European unemployment.[13] In this view, the inflow of foreign workers weakens union power, with a negative impact on wages and a beneficial effect on natives' employment.[14] In short, the "presence of unemployment is not an argument per se against migration."[15]

Thus far the discussion has focused on the impact of immigration on the labor market, with no mention of other possible benefits and costs stemming from the inflow of foreign workers. Yet one of the most charged issues in the debate about foreign workers in the United States is whether migrants "pay their way" in the welfare system. One analyst has shown that migrants are more likely than

11. Zweimuller and Winter-Ebmer (1996).
12. De New and Zimmermann (1994).
13. OECD (1995).
14. Schmidt, Stilz, and Zimmermann (1994).
15. Zimmermann (1995b). In this setting, governments can act strategically. By allowing more foreign workers they can weaken union power enough so as to induce a fall in the unskilled wage with a beneficial effect on natives' employment. The realism of this model is clearly worth investigating. The results appear to be sensitive to the way union wage-setting strategies and government immigration policies interact. Suppose, for instance, that unions set the wage in advance of government migration policy. Then the influence of migration in moderating union wage demands may vanish. Higher wages would still lead to a fall in labor demand. The resulting increase in unemployment however would presumably deter governments from pursuing a more permissive immigration policy.

natives to rely on the welfare system and receive on average larger payments than natives.[16] Moreover, migrants "assimilate" into the welfare system; that is, their propensity to rely on welfare payments increases with their length of stay in the host country. At the same time, migrants pay taxes whose receipts are significantly larger than the welfare payments they receive. Do migrants therefore provide a positive contribution to public finances? There is no definite answer: taxes are used not only to pay for the welfare and schooling programs that migrants use but also for other public goods, and it is virtually impossible to determine how expenses on, say, national parks, police, and defense increase with the arrival of new migrants.

The federal nature of U.S. institutions adds to the problem. U.S. states are in large part responsible for welfare payments but receive a disproportionately low share of tax revenues. Therefore if immigrants tend to concentrate in a given state, the latter's public finances will suffer. This is the problem in California and the economic motivation behind Proposition 187. These issues have received scant attention in Europe, despite the greater generosity of the European welfare system. But notice that the "California problem" is not an issue at a pan-European level, because of the low share of public spending and taxes channeled through EU institutions, or at an intranational level, to the extent that national rather than regional governments in Europe are responsible for welfare payments. Matters may change in the near future, however, because of the growth in EU institutions, on the one hand, and the trend toward fiscal federalism at the country level, on the other. Both trends will complicate the task of defining a common immigration policy at the European level.

The impacts on the labor market and on the public finance situation do not exhaust the list of potential items on the cost-benefit balance sheet of immigration. Another benefit that economists are often keen to emphasize is that an inflow of foreign workers will increase gross domestic product by more than the migrants' wage bill, even if migrants are paid the value of their marginal product. Immigration, in other words, yields an immigration surplus to the host country. The higher the initial share of foreign workers and the more

16. Borjas (1994). This is no longer true, however, once we control for individual characteristics (Borjas, 1994). Therefore, migrants are not per se more likely to rely on welfare, but have less favorable individual characteristics that on average increase the probability that they will participate in a welfare program.

pronounced the fall in domestic wages, the greater this surplus will be. Somewhat paradoxically the greater the impact of immigration on the labor market, the more beneficial the overall welfare effect of additional foreign workers.[17] The extent of this welfare gain is hard to gauge. For the benefits of immigration, estimates range from about 0.1 percent of GDP[18] to somewhat higher levels.[19] There is some reason to believe, however, that aggregate estimates undervalue the contribution of migration to domestic welfare to the extent that they cannot capture the sectoral distortions and the sectoral bottlenecks that restrictions on the flow of workers entail. A similar argument is often made in connection with trade policies.[20] Clearly, this issue requires more research.

Are There Too Many Migrants?

Existing evidence seems to suggest that immigration has a limited impact on the labor market situation in Europe, including the wage and employment conditions of unskilled workers. Similarly, there seem to be few reasons for concern about the public finance effects of immigration. Yet most European countries consider migration a problem. After 1989 newspapers were filled with stories of aggression against foreigners, episodes of racial intolerance and discrimination, and the like. Since then policymakers have been busily trying to implement more restrictive migration policies, limiting asylum requests, for instance, in an effort to defuse social tensions and stem the growth of right-wing, racist-motivated political parties.

One reason for the anti-immigrant climate in Europe may be that Europeans, unlike Americans, do not see their land as one built on immigration. In the case of Germany, citizenship is tied to ethnicity. Ethnic Germans have a constitutional right to German citizenship even though they may have never lived in Germany and are unaware of its social, cultural, and linguistic traditions. Conversely, immigrants may have spent their whole life on German land but are not

17. There is no paradox. Migration benefits the host country by making labor less scarce and raising the return to capital. The gains to capitalists outweigh the losses to wage earners.
18. Borjas (1995).
19. Bauer and Zimmermann (1995).
20. Feenstra (1992).

TABLE 5-3. *Attitudes toward Immigrants, 1991–93*

Percentage of all answers

Answer	Belgium	Denmark	Germany	Greece	Spain	France
Too many	54.3	44.0	56.7	43.7	24.3	54.7
A lot but not too many	33.0	36.0	34.0	41.7	33.5	33.7
Not many	5.7	17.0	4.7	7.3	31.8	5.7
Does not know	7.0	3.0	4.6	7.3	10.4	5.9

	Ireland	Portugal	Nether-lands	Luxem-bourg	United Kingdom	Italy
Too many	10.3	23.7	46.7	24.3	51.3	64.0
A lot but not too many	25.0	39.0	40.7	48.3	31.7	28.7
Not many	53.3	22.7	8.0	20.0	11.0	4.7
Does not know	10.4	14.6	4.6	7.4	6.0	2.6

Source: Eurobarometre (L'opinion publique dans l'Union Européenne).

entitled to German citizenship. One implication of this attitude is that immigration will be well tolerated and will not stir excessive cultural and social tensions if it is for the most part temporary. This was indeed the case, as mentioned earlier, in the 1960s. When the nature of immigration changed in the 1970s and 1980s, with new migrants staying permanently rather than on a temporary basis, the perception of immigration changed as well. Furthermore, it seems that the attitude toward migration is now determined mostly by cultural and social country-specific factors and do not correlate strongly with the economic conditions at home.

A survey conducted by the European Commission (the so-called Euro-barometer) sheds some light on this issue. The survey contains several questions about European attitudes toward immigrants. Respondents were asked whether there are (a) too many, (b) a lot, but not too many, or (c) not a lot of immigrants. Table 5-3 shows the distribution of the different answers for twelve EU countries. According to the results of the survey, a majority of citizens in Belgium, Germany, France, Italy, and the United Kingdom believe there are too many migrants; those in Spain, Ireland, Luxembourg, and Portugal say there are a lot, but not too many; and those in Denmark, Greece, and the Netherlands fall somewhere in between, somewhat closer to the first group. The figures in table 5-3 are averages for 1991–93. Attitudes did not seem to change much during this period, at least not in the direction of being more favorable to immigrants. If anything, they grew more negative.

Are these attitudes related in any way to objective factors, such as the presence of foreigners and the level of unemployment? Or do they simply reflect cultural and social prejudices, in particular the fact that Europe is not seen as a land of immigration? These issues can be investigated by relating the share of most negative attitudes ("there are too many migrants") to the country's unemployment rates (figure 5-7) and to the population share of foreigners (figure 5-8). The results of this exercise indicate that the link is quite weak and, if anything, goes in the wrong direction. A high population share of foreigners is not associated with a more negative attitude toward migrants. Similarly, high unemployment at home does not seem to affect the attitude toward foreigners. If the share of those who believe that there are too many migrants is regressed on the actual population share of foreigners, the unemployment rate, and a set of country intercepts, only the latter are found to play a significant role. This result can be interpreted as an indication that economic factors do not greatly affect the attitude toward migration, which is instead determined primarily by country-specific motives.

Which Migration Policies for Europe?

Thus far the discussion has shown that the potential flow of immigration toward the more developed part of Europe is quite large, particularly from North Africa. Barring catastrophic events, Eastern European migration should be quite limited in size. Yet, as a whole, the potential for massive migration pressure toward Europe should not be overlooked. Another significant point is that the inhabitants of Europe do not consider it to be a land of immigration. In the main, attitudes toward immigrants are shaped by cultural and social factors rather than by economic considerations.

The New Challenges

Perhaps the biggest challenge for policymakers is to regulate migration so as to satisfy the demand for foreign workers. At the same time, they must avoid excessive migrations, which could be

FIGURE 5-7. *Attitude toward Immigration and Unemployment Rates in Host Countries*

Percent

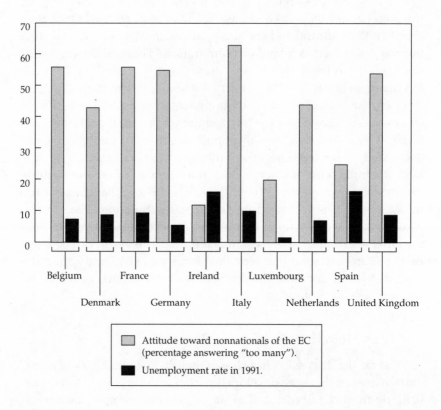

Belgium   France   Ireland   Luxembourg   Spain

Denmark   Germany   Italy   Netherlands   United Kingdom

☐ Attitude toward nonnationals of the EC (percentage answering "too many").

■ Unemployment rate in 1991.

politically destabilizing. The demand for migrant workers—though not as high as in the 1960s—is likely to continue, particularly in the informal sector and in unskilled, labor-intensive activities. Restrictive migration policies may have a stifling effect on some sectors of the economy and in the end are likely to foster illegal immigration. Conversely, an excessively lax immigration policy would face strong social and political opposition. In short, policymakers have two options. One, the so-called control approach, advocates tighter controls on Europe's external borders, viewing such policy as the only way to stem undesired migration. In this approach, the supply of unskilled migrants (skilled migrants are generally not seen as a problem) is potentially infinite

FIGURE 5-8. *Attitude toward Immigration and the Stock of Foreign Population*

Percent

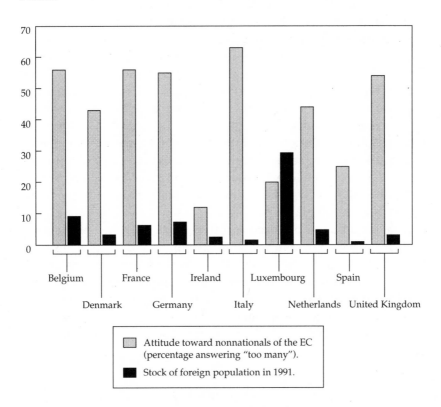

Belgium	France	Ireland	Luxembourg	Spain	
Denmark	Germany	Italy	Netherlands	United Kingdom	

☐ Attitude toward nonnationals of the EC (percentage answering "too many").

■ Stock of foreign population in 1991.

(in economic jargon, it is infinitely elastic). Only effective controls will enable European countries to avoid massive and undesired immigration. In contrast, advocates of the so-called developmental approach emphasize the porousness of controls. European borders cannot be sealed off. Would-be Polish migrants set to cross the Oder River and move into Germany can do so as easily as Mexican migrants ready to cross the Rio Grande and try their fortune in the United States. In this view, migration controls act as a wire-mesh screen. They can slow the flow of migration, but they cannot stop it, particularly if outside pressure is too high. According to the developmental approach, therefore, the main priority of policymakers should be to eliminate, or at least alleviate, the conditions that prompt people to emigrate by promoting sustained and equitable growth in the sending country.

The difference between the two approaches is mainly one of timing and should not be overemphasized. Advocates of the developmental approach do not deny the need to maintain immigration controls in the transition period before development policies become effective in alleviating the migration pressure in sending regions. They stress, however, that short-run concerns about controlling migration have too often diverted policymakers from the basic causes of migration pressure in poor countries. Conversely, most supporters of the control approach acknowledge the ineffectiveness of controls as a long-run tool to stem immigration but argue that it can be decades before economic growth in the sending regions can affect the propensity to emigrate. Controls therefore are likely to be in place for a long period, and policy should be designed to render them more effective. Both control and development policies are therefore essential. Which approach should be emphasized will then depend on the link between economic development in the sending country and the propensity to emigrate. If income growth in the sending countries brings only a modest reduction in the propensity to emigrate, then control will have to play a central role in the design of migration policies. Conversely, if economic development in the sending country is an effective way to limit migration, then it should become the top priority of migration policies.

The Role of "Developmental" Policies

Studies of migration patterns in Mexico[21] and Southern Europe[22] have found that economic development in the sending country is a very effective means of reducing migration flows in the long run, but that it can take quite a while to become effective and may even be "counterproductive" in the short run.[23] The reason for this is that economic development brings a reallocation of resources that is often associated with a disruption in old production modes and the uproot-

21. Stanton and Teitelbaum (1992).
22. Faini and Venturini (1994).
23. Notice though that the causality may also run the opposite way, with migration affecting income growth in the sending country both by alleviating excess labor supply and by fostering saving through remittances.

ing of a portion of the rural population. These factors are conducive to more rather than less migration. Moreover, economic development improves the flow of information about job opportunities abroad and allows would-be migrants to finance the cost of migrating abroad. Thus there are good reasons to believe that for relatively poor countries income and wage growth at home may lead to an increase rather than a fall in migration. Fortunately, this pattern will not last forever. The disruption attendant on fast economic growth will subside. Falling wage and income gaps vis-à-vis the receiving regions will then discourage migration.

Economic growth in the sending country may even lead to an accelerated decline in the rate of migration.[24] Consider what happens when (international) migration is costly not only in monetary terms, but also in terms of lost social relationships, the adjustment to a new and unfamiliar milieu, and the difficulties of adapting to different cultural and linguistic traditions. Individuals have roots and, everything else being equal, would rather live in their own country. When income grows at home, then, *even if the income differential with the receiving regions is unchanged,* individuals will be keener to consume the amenities of their home region and will therefore be less willing to migrate. In the end, the relationship between home income and migration will have a reverse-U shape. For relatively poor countries, income increases will foster migration. For richer countries, higher income will be associated with falling migration. That is to say,

> After a certain point, further growth in the origin countries will lead to lower migration propensity, even with constant wage differentials. Put . . . differently, higher income in the sending countries will lower migrations both through their impact on the income differential and because it will lower the propensity to move abroad. . . . [S]uch effects will not work for relatively poor countries, where income growth may be associated with more rather than less migrations.[25]

In this study, data for three Southern European countries (Greece, Portugal, and Turkey) have been pooled with information on Mexico. The countries of North Africa are not included because the time-

24. Faini and Venturini (1994).
25. Faini and Venturini (1994).

series on migration there is not of sufficient length. It is then possible to compute the turning point in the income-migration link, that is, the income level after which further increases in income will lead to an accelerated reduction in the rate of migration. Standard econometric tests showed that it was not possible to impose the constraint of an equal turning point for Mexico and the three European countries. When a separate turning point was estimated, a value of $3,700 (in 1985 international prices) was calculated for Greece, Portugal, and Turkey and $4,500 for Mexico.

These results can be used to predict the impact of income growth in the countries of North Africa, provided that one is willing to believe that they apply to these countries as well. For countries whose income level is below $3,700, income growth would most likely have a perverse effect on the propensity to migrate. For countries whose income per capita is above $4,500, further income growth will have a strongly negative effect on the rate of migration. Data from other studies suggest that Mexico, with a per capita income of $5,379 in 1990, lies well to the right of the turning point in the income-migration relationship. North Africa, where incomes in 1990 ranged from $2,021 in Morocco to $2,860 in Tunisia, still has some way to go before it reaches the income level after which the propensity to migrate will decline. Developmental policies therefore are quite effective in the case of Mexico and the United States. For Europe, however, it may be a while before such policies can become the main instrument of migration policies.

Trade Policies

If developmental policies are less than fully effective and controls are bound to be porous, what are the alternatives for Europe's policymakers? Trade policies are often mentioned. Trade liberalization between sending and receiving countries should have substantial effects on migration flows. This is indeed a time-honored proposition in trade theory, which holds that commodity trade and factor movements are substitutes, so that trade liberalization should reduce the incentives for factor mobility. In the traditional trade model, labor-abundant countries will export those commodities that use labor in a relatively intensive way. Imports will instead be concentrated in more capital-intensive activities. The expansion in both exports and imports attendant on trade liberalization should then boost the demand for labor (the abundant factor) and reduce the demand for capital (the scarce factor). Conversely, in the capital-abundant country, the demand for labor will fall and the demand for capital will increase. Trade therefore makes the scarce (abundant) factor less scarce (abundant). The price of the scarce factor (labor in the industrialized country, capital in the developing country) would then be expected to fall, the price of the abundant factor to rise. As a result of commodity trade, therefore, factor prices will tend to converge between countries. The reduction (in the limit, the elimination) of factor price differentials will in turn reduce the incentive for factor mobility, as claimed.

Trade liberalization tends to discourage factor movements for other reasons as well. First, a more liberal trade regime may foster growth in sending countries.[26] Second, it should increase the demand for labor in these countries for given output growth and therefore boost the employment intensity of growth. Third, it will encourage the downsizing of labor-intensive importable sectors in receiving countries and thereby reduce the demand for migrant labor. All these factors should help to alleviate migration pressure.

Unfortunately, evidence on the link between trade and migration is limited, although some researchers have found that trade liberalization between Mexico and the United States would have a significant discouraging effect on Mexican migration.[27] Others find that unilateral trade liberalization would boost labor demand in Morocco by shifting activity toward exportable sectors.[28] It has also been shown that the share of foreign workers is positively related to sectoral import penetration and negatively related to both export orientation and the comparative advantage measure (table 5-4). Migrants therefore tend to concentrate in import-competing sectors and are underrepresented in export-oriented sectors. This is consistent with the notion that receiving countries have a comparative advantage in skilled and capital-intensive sectors. Migrants, who are for the most part unskilled, will

26. World Bank (1990).
27. Hill and Mendez (1984).
28. Faini and de Melo (1995). Indirect evidence is reported in Abowd and Freeman (1991) and in Faini and Venturini (1993). Both studies look at the employment share of foreign workers for several sectors in receiving countries and relate it to a number of sectoral trade measures: export orientation, import penetration, and a measure of revealed comparative advantage. We report their results for France, Germany, and the United States and extend them to Italy and Switzerland.

TABLE 5-4. *Correlation Coefficients between the Sectoral Share of Foreign Workers and Main Trade Indicators* [a]

Country	X/Y	M/(Y + M – X)	(X – M)/(X + M)
United States	–0.16	0.22	–0.30
Germany	–0.08	. . .	. . .
France	–0.17	0.40	–0.43
Spain	–0.05	0.02	–0.20
Switzerland	0.55	0.77	–0.43
Italy	0.05	0.07	–0.12

a. X = exports; M = imports; Y = gross output; X/Y = export orientation; M/(Y + M – X) = import penetration (as a share of domestic demand); and (X – M)/(X + M) = revealed comparative advantage.

then tend to concentrate in import-competing sectors where demand for low-skilled labor is greater. Trade protection will have a twofold effect: first, it will strengthen the pull factors of migration by boosting output in import-competing sectors that rely to a larger extent on migrant labor; second, it will discourage the growth of labor-intensive exports in sending countries, depress employment prospects, and reinforce the push elements of migration. On both counts, therefore, trade liberalization could alleviate migration pressure. Interestingly, the North American Free Trade Agreement has often been justified by the desire to reduce migration. As President Carlos Salinas put it, "Mexico wants to export goods, not people."

European policymakers have been less enthusiastic than their U.S. counterparts about trade liberalization with their poorer neighbors. On paper, trade between Europe and North Africa is not subject to many restrictions. Yet a careful analysis shows that several barriers to exports from North Africa still exist.[29] Even the successful negotiation of the Euro-Maghreb agreements between the European Union and Morocco and Tunisia did not prompt substantial liberalization on the EU side. The restrictive stance by European policymakers in the trade field was to some extent compensated by a relatively generous financial protocol, with the European Union committing itself to partly support the costs of the adjustment process in the Maghreb countries. The strategy of trading off concessions against promises of financial assistance is a recurring feature of EU policy toward the third

29. Hoekman and Djankov (1996).

world.[30] The European Union has often been criticized, rightly so, for pursuing such a strategy on the grounds that trade is a better means of strengthening the production capabilities of developing countries than aid.

The reason for the restrictive EU stance in the trade field lies in the high share of "sensitive" exports of Tunisia and Morocco to the European Union. Agricultural goods and textiles, which are two highly sensitive sectors in Europe, account for 70 percent and 65 percent of total exports for the two Maghreb countries, respectively. Furthermore, this fraction has been growing rapidly since 1983. More farsightedness on the part of European governments would be required to acknowledge the link between trade and migration and to afford the short-run costs of adjusting to greater import competition in exchange for greater economic and political stability on their southern border. Unlike their counterparts in the United States, European policymakers seem less willing to accept that migration policies cannot be formulated independently of other policy choices. They should acknowledge, however, that Europe cannot close its border to both goods and people from developing countries.

Improving the Coordination of Europe's Migration Policies

Europe has had difficulty forging a coherent set of migration policies in large part because of lack of coordination among EU governments. Member states have strenuously resisted all attempts by the European Commission to have a greater say in migration matters. When the European Court of Justice ruled in favor of the Commission, member governments tried to circumvent the decision by launching a number of initiatives on migration that lay outside EU institutions. The Schengen Agreement in particular, which envisages the abolition of all border controls for travel between participating countries, was not an EU but an intergovernmental initiative that does not include a number of EU countries, namely, Denmark, the United Kingdom, and Ireland. Still, as the Maastricht Treaty makes clear, the decisionmaking power of the Commission on migration matters is bound to increase. First, migration is likely to affect the orderly working of the single market. Second, the abolition of internal border controls requires the implementation of a common migration policy. The stakes are high, however. The ques-

30. Grilli (1993).

tion of who is entitled to migrate is linked to the granting of citizenship rights. Member states would be uncomfortable relinquishing this sovereign power to a supranational institution such as the Commission, which could one day be empowered to determine whether Hong Kong refugees or Macao citizens should be allowed to enter the EU. Moreover, a common migration policy may face the same problem as in the United States, where the citizens of one region (that is, California) feel they are bearing a disproportionate burden of immigration costs. Finally, Northern European countries fear that the abolition of internal border controls could encourage external migration, with would-be migrants using Southern European countries (where controls are supposedly weaker) as a stepping-stone for migrating toward northern destinations. These fears have resulted in delays in implementing the Schengen Agreement.

These problems are not without a solution. There is little evidence that, in the wake of the abolition of internal border controls, northern countries will be flooded by immigrants from the South. First, Southern European countries have become an attractive destination for immigrants from North Africa, because of both geographical proximity and the larger size of the informal sector. Second, econometric evidence does not indicate that the rise of new destinations in Southern Europe during the 1980s should be attributed to the implementation of highly restrictive immigration policies in Northern Europe.[31] Finally, a common migration policy could be designed to allow individual countries to retain full sovereign power on sensitive matters. While the costs of a common migration policy are likely to be limited, its benefits are easier to gauge. In particular, the fact that migration policies are formulated at a national level whereas trade choices are made at the EU level precludes effective coordination between the two sets of policies. The trend toward the definition of a common migration policy at the European level seems difficult to reverse.

Migration Policies and Prospects: A U.S.-European Comparison

Europe and the United States share many features as far as migration is concerned. In both, immigration has become a divisive social

31. Faini (1995).

and political issue and stands high on the political agenda. In both, policymakers are concerned that political and economic instability in their relatively poorer neighbors to the South may result in massive and undesired population flows. Finally, both Europe and the United States have recently signed trade agreements with their southern neighbors with a view to stemming migration pressures, yet they are still debating the relative merits of control versus developmental approaches to the migration problem.

Although the similarities between the United States and Europe are impressive, the differences are equally striking. First of all, they differ in the nature of their concern about the economic impact of migration. Unlike the United States, European countries (with the exception of the United Kingdom) have not experienced a significant deterioration in the pattern of income distribution and have avoided a fall in the purchasing power of the lowest wages. To a large extent, however, preserving a relatively egalitarian pattern of earning distribution has come at the expense of growing unemployment, particularly among low-skilled workers. It is revealing that during the 1980s Europe's unemployment rate for workers with only a basic education increased at a much faster rate than overall unemployment. In Europe, therefore, the main concern is the employment impact of further migration. The United States, on the other hand, has not experienced a steady rise in the unemployment rate, but rather a deterioration in the pattern of income distribution. Its main policy concern is therefore the impact of migration on wages, particularly of unskilled workers.

Existing wisdom attributes the different pattern of wages and employment between Europe and the United States to the fact that in Europe minimum wage regulations, union power, and other labor market institutions have helped to avoid a marked fall in the unskilled wage, at the expense, however, of growing unemployment. Surprisingly, the (limited) empirical evidence for Europe seems to suggest that the main impact of migration has been on wages rather than employment. One possible explanation stresses the possibility that more migration may have a strong disciplining effect on union behavior, thereby inducing greater wage moderation and allowing faster employment growth. In the United States, excessive union power is less of an issue, and empirical studies have found it more difficult to identify a substantial effect of migration on either wages or employment of natives.

European and U.S. concerns about migration differ even more markedly in the area of fiscal policy. Whether migrants "pay their way" into the welfare system has become a highly charged issue in U.S. political circles but is not of much concern in Europe. This is surprising given the greater generosity of the European welfare system; it should be recalled, however, that the weakness of federal institutions in Europe allows for a better geographical matching of the taxes migrants pay and the benefits they receive. The California problem is unlikely to arise in this context; further progress on the road toward economic and political integration in Europe should not lead to any radical change in this regard.

Europe and the United States also differ in the extent to which each region faces a "migration threat." Both demographic and economic factors indicate that migration pressure of North Africa on Europe is significantly larger than that of Mexico on the United States. For instance, Morocco's real GDP per capita in 1990 was less than 15 percent of that in France. In the same year, the ratio between Mexican and U.S. real GDP per capita was almost 30 percent. Moreover, the real per capita income differential between Mexico and the United States is not too different from that observed between Southern and Northern Europe in the late 1960s, that is, a decade before Southern European countries had completed their migration transition and had become the target of immigration flows. Whether Mexico will follow the same route is difficult to say. To judge from Europe's experience, however, the probability of such an event will depend to a large extent on whether economic ties between Mexico and the United States grow sufficiently strong. It is indeed an accepted fact that European integration favored income and wage convergence and the latter was instrumental in discouraging internal migration.[32]

In addition to fostering convergence, income growth in the sending country may have further effects on the propensity to migrate. As noted earlier, even with unchanged wage and income differentials, growth in the sending countries may affect the propensity to migrate: more precisely, the propensity to migrate follows an inverse U-pattern, rising first with income and declining later. Econometric evidence seems to suggest that Mexico lies well to the right of this turning point; further income growth should therefore be associ-

32. Ben-David (1993).

ated with a significant fall in migration pressure. Overall, there are good reasons to believe that migration pressure from Mexico to the United States should subside, provided of course that Mexico's economic and political stability can be preserved.

The picture changes somewhat in the case of North African migration to Europe. The income (and wage) gaps between sending countries in North Africa and destination countries in Europe are substantial. Demographic projections indicate that the absolute size of the more mobile cohorts will double in the next thirty years. It is true that rising income may mitigate the pressure to migrate, but for North African countries, the evidence is less reassuring. Their present income level lies to the left of the turning point. Even if they grow at a very respectable annual rate of 3 percent, Tunisia and Morocco will reach the (lower) turning point only in 2000 and in 2010, respectively. In the meantime, therefore, European policymakers have little option but to rely on controls. Yet they should not lose sight of the fact that migration controls can work in the short run but are bound to be ineffective in the medium run, particularly if migration pressure is high. The formulation of long-run strategies to deal with the migration issue cannot be postponed simply because of the pressing need to implement short-run controls. It is true that the internal organization of European societies, in particular the widespread use of identity cards, makes the implementation of immigration controls easier. Yet this factor has not played a crucial role in stemming inflows and ensuring the effectiveness of controls, as witnessed, for instance, by the very large size of the illegal foreign population in Italy and Spain. Moreover, European societies have become increasingly multiracial and multicultural. It is unlikely that they would tolerate all the restrictions on personal freedom that would be required for controls to become the only or main instrument of immigration policy.

Conclusions

European migration policies face several challenges. The two-pronged approach based on the assimilation of existing migrants and the implementation of tight border controls to prevent further migration seems gravely inadequate in the present situation. This approach neglects the fact that the demand for foreign labor is still a crucial determinant of migratory flows. The demand for migrant labor is indeed likely to be sustained, both in the tertiary sector and in import-competing industries. In addition, controls cannot be waterproof. European borders are too porous to withstand the pressure of both migrant supply and the demand for foreign workers.

Policies are not formulated in a vacuum but reflect the aspirations, influences, and fears of voters and pressure groups. Migration policies are not different in this respect from other policies. The crucial fact is that attitudes toward migration have changed markedly and for the worse in Europe since the late 1960s. Matters would perhaps be easier if the negative attitude toward migration could be attributed to economic factors. Then one might hope that improved economic conditions in receiving countries would bring a less prejudiced stance toward migration. Unfortunately, the results of this study suggest that economic considerations play a limited role in affecting attitudes toward migration. Cost-benefit calculations show that the economic impact of foreign workers on the labor market or public finance conditions is too small to shape attitudes toward foreign workers. Furthermore, public opinion toward migration seems to be motivated in large part by country-specific considerations, most likely cultural and social factors. The labor market situation or the actual size of the foreign population plays an altogether negligible role. One worrisome implication of this is that the attitude toward migration would not change much even if labor market conditions in Europe experienced a marked improvement and the unemployment rate fell to more acceptable levels.

Policymakers in Europe are therefore left with few options. In the short run they will be forced to rely on migration controls, despite the fact that these might be less than fully effective. However, concerns about migration controls should not distract policymakers from the urgent task of addressing the ultimate causes of migration pressure from poor countries. Both developmental policies and trade liberalization can be effective means of reducing migration pressure on Europe's southern border. The fact that these policy instruments will work mostly in the medium run should be an incentive to rely on them at the earliest opportunity, certainly not a justification for a further delay in their implementation. In the meantime, migration policy will have to strike a balance between the demand for foreign labor in receiving countries, the desire to limit the social and political implications of "excessive" population flows, and the growing migration pressure originating in the third world. After all, arguing that Europe is not a land of immigration and that immigration controls can be waterproof is simply a means of fostering illegal immigration. A braver stance would be to recognize that Europe will remain the destination of many would-be migrants and to allow some of them to enter legally each year. Immigration permits could then be auctioned off or awarded through a lottery system. These are some of the challenges that await the formulation of Europe's migration policy both at the EU and at the national level.

References

Abowd, John M., and Richard B. Freeman. 1991. "Introduction and Summary." In *Immigration, Trade and the Labor Market*, edited by John Abowd and Richard Freeman. University of Chicago Press.

Albert, Michel. 1991. *Capitalisme contre Capitalisme*. Paris: Seuil.

Allen, Franklin. 1993. Stock Markets and Resource Allocation." In *Capital Markets and Financial Intermediation*, edited by Colin Mayer and Xavier Vives. Cambridge University Press.

Arthur, W. Brian. 1988. "Self-Reinforcing Mechanisms in Economics." In *The Economy as an Evolving Complex System*, edited by P. W. Anderson, K. J. Arrow, and D. Pines, 9–31. New York: Addison-Wesley.

Audretsch, David. 1989. "Legalized Cartels in West Germany." *Antitrust Bulletin* 34 (Fall).

Baldwin, Richard E., and Joseph F. Francois. 1996. "Transatlantic Free Trade: A Quantitative Assessment." London: Centre for Economic Policy Research.

Bauer, Michel, and Bénédicte Bertin-Mourot. 1992. "L'Etat, le capital et l'entreprise au sommet des grandes entreprises." "Les 200" Comparison Franco-Allemande. *La Revue de l'IRES* (10).

Bauer, Thomas, and Klaus F. Zimmermann. 1995. "Integrating the East: The Labour Market Effects of Immigration." Discussion Paper 1235. London: Centre for Economic Policy Research.

Bayoumi, Tamim, and Barry Eichengreen. 1996. "Optimum Currency Areas and Exchange Rate Variability: Theory and Evidence Compared." Washington, D.C.: International Monetary Fund.

Ben-David, Ben. 1993. "Equalizing Exchange: Trade Liberalization and Income Convergence." *Quarterly Journal of Economics* 108 (August): 653–79.

Berghahn, Volker, and Karsten Detlev. 1987. *Industrial Relations in West Germany*. Oxford: Berg.

Bergsten, C. Fred. 1996. "Globalizing Free Trade." *Foreign Affairs (U.S.)* 75 (3): 105–20.

Bergsten, C. Fred, and C. Randall Henning. 1996. *Global Economic Leadership and the Group of Seven.* Washington, D.C.: Institute for International Economics.

Bolton, Patrick, and Mathias Dewatripont. 1994. "The Firm as a Communication Network." *Quarterly Journal of Economics* 109 (November): 809–39.

Borjas, George J. 1994. "Immigration and Welfare, 1970–1990." Working Paper 4872. Cambridge, Mass.: National Bureau of Economic Research.

___. 1995. "The Economic Benefits from Immigration." *Journal of Economic Perspectives* 9 (2): 3–22.

Bryant, Ralph C. 1987. "Intergovernmental Coordination of Economic Policies: An Interim Stocktaking." In *International Monetary Cooperation: Essays in Honor of Henry C. Wallich,* edited by Peter B. Kenen. Essays in International Finance 169. Princeton University, Department of Economics, International Finance Section.

Bryant, Ralph C., and others. 1988. *Empirical Macroeconomics for Interdependent Economies.* Brookings.

Buiter, Willem, Giancarlo Corsetti, and Paolo Pesenti. 1996. "Interpreting the ERM Crisis: Country-Specific and Systemic Issues." Discussion Paper 1466. Princeton University.

Carlin, Wendy, and David Soskice. 1997. "Shocks to the System: The German Political Economy under Stress." *National Institute Economic Review* 159 (January): 57–76.

Casper, Steven. 1996. "German Industrial Associations and the Diffusion of Innovative Economic Organization." Discussion Paper 96-306. Berlin: WZB.

Centre for Economic Policy Research (CEPR). 1995. *Flexible Integration: Towards a More Effective and Democratic Europe.* London: CEPR.

Collinson, Sarah. 1993. *Europe and International Migration.* London: Pinter.

Commission of the European Communities, Directorate-General for Economic and Financial Affairs. 1993. "The ERM in 1992." *European Economy* 54: 141–57.

Committee of Governors of the Central Banks of the Member States of the European Economic Community. 1993. *Annual Report 1992.* Basle: Committee of Governors.

Cooper, Richard, Barry Eichengreen, Gerald Holtham, Robert Putnam, and C. Randall Henning. 1989. *Can Nations Agree? Issues in International Economic Cooperation.* Brookings.

Crockett, Andrew. 1989. "The Role of International Institutions in Surveillance and Policy Coordination." In *Macroeconomic Policies in an Interdependent World,* edited by Ralph Bryant, David Currie, Jacob Frenkel, Paul Masson, and Richard Portes, 343–64. Washington, D.C.: International Monetary Fund.

Crouch, Colin, and Wolfgang Streeck, eds. 1995. *Modern Capitalism or Modern Capitalisms?* London: Francis Pinter.

Culpepper, David H. 1996. "Problems on the Road to `High Skill': A Sectoral Lesson from the Transfer of the Dual System of Vocational Training to Eastern Germany." Discussion Paper 96-317. Berlin: WZB.

De New, John P., and Klaus F. Zimmermann. 1994. "Native Wage Impact of Foreign Labour: A Random Effects Panel Analysis." Discussion Paper 851. London: Centre for Economic Policy Research.

Eichengreen, Barry. 1992. "Should the Maastricht Treaty Be Saved?" *Princeton Studies in International Finance* 74. Princeton University, Department of Economics, International Finance Section.

____. 1993. *Reconstructing Europe's Trade and Payments: The European Payments Union.* Manchester: Manchester University Press.

____. 1994. *International Monetary Arrangements for the 21st Century.* Brookings.

____. 1997. "The Changing Nature of International Monetary and Financial Cooperation." Washington, D.C.: International Monetary Fund.

Eichengreen, Barry, and Fabio Ghironi. 1996. "European Monetary Unification: The Challenges Ahead." In *Monetary Reform in Europe,* edited by Francisco Torres, 83–120. Lisbon: Universidade Católica Editora.

Eichengreen, Barry, and Richard Portes. 1996. "Managing the Next Mexico." University of California, Berkeley.

Eichengreen, Barry, and Jürgen von Hagen. 1996. "Fiscal Policy and Monetary Union: Federalism, Fiscal Restrictions and the No-Bailout Rule." In *Monetary Policy in an Integrated World Economy,* edited by Horst Siebert, 211–31. Tübingen: J. C. B. Mohr.

Emminger, Otmar. 1986. *D-Mark, Dollar, Wahrungskrisen.* Stuttgart: Deutsch Verlags-Anstalt.

European Community, the Commission. 1995. *Thirteenth Annual Report from the Commission to the European Parliament on The Community's Anti-Dumping and Anti-Subsidy Activities (1994).* Document COM(95)309. Brussels.

Faini, Riccardo. 1995. "Migration in the Integrated EU." In *Expanding Membership of the European Union,* edited by R. Baldwin, P. Haaparanta, and J. Kiander. Cambridge University Press.

———. 1996. "European Migrants: An Endangered Species?" Centre for Economic Policy Research Conference on Regional Integration, La Coruna, Spain.

Faini, Riccardo, and Jaime de Melo 1995. "Trade Liberalization, Employment and Migration: Some Simulations for Morocco." Discussion Paper 1198. London: Centre for Economic Policy Research.

Faini, Riccardo, and Alissandra Venturini. 1993. "Labour Migration in Europe: Trade, Aid and Migration: Some Basic Policy Issues." *European Economic Review* 37: 435–42.

———. 1994. "Migrations and Growth: The Experience of Southern Europe." Discussion Paper 964. London: Centre for Economic Policy Research.

Farrell, Joseph, and Robert Gibbons. 1989. "Cheap Talk Can Matter in Bargaining." *Journal of Economic Theory* 48 (June): 221–37.

Feenstra, Robert C. 1992. "How Costly Is Protectionism?" *Journal of Economic Perspectives* 6 (3): 159–78.

Ferenczi, Imre, and Walter Francis Willcox. 1931. *International Migrations.* Geneva: United Nations.

Frankel, Jeffrey A. 1988. "Obstacles to International Economic Policy Coordination." *Princeton Studies in International Finance* 64, Princeton University, Department of Economics, International Finance Section.

———. 1990. "Obstacles to Coordination, and a Consideration of Two Proposals to Overcome Them: International Nominal Targeting (INT) and the Hosomi Fund." In *Macroeconomic Policies in an Interdependent World,* edited by Ralph Bryant, David Currie, Jacob Frenkel, Paul Masson, and Richard Portes, 109–44. Washington, D.C.: International Monetary Fund.

———. 1997. *Regional Trading Blocs in the World Economic System.* Washington, D.C.: Institute for International Economics.

Frankel, Jeffrey A., and Katherine E. Rockett. 1988. "International Macroeconomic Policy Coordination When Policymakers Do Not Agree on the True Model." *American Economic Review* 78 (June): 318–40.

Franks, Julian, and Colin Mayer. 1990. "Capital Markets and Corporate Control: A Study of France, Germany and the UK." *Economic Policy* 5 (1): 191–231.

Friedberg, Rachel M., and Jennifer Hunt. 1995. "The Impact of Immigration on Host Country Wages, Employment and Growth." *Journal of Economic Perspectives* 9 (2): 23–44.

Fudenberg, Drew, and Eric Maskin. 1986. "The Folk Theorem in Repeated Games with Discounting and Incomplete Information." *Econometrica* 54(May):533–54.

Ghironi, Fabio, and Barry Eichengreen. 1995. "U.S.-Europe Policy Interactions from the Post–Bretton Woods Era to EMU." University of California, Berkeley.

Goldstein, Judith. 1988. "Ideas, Institutions, and American Trade Policy." *International Organization* 42 (Winter): 179–217.

Grilli, Enzo R. 1993. *The European Community and the Developing Countries.* Cambridge University Press.

Gros, Daniel, and Niels Thygesen. 1991. *European Monetary Integration from the European Monetary System to the European Monetary Union.* London: Macmillan.

Haas, Peter M. 1992. "Introduction: Epistemic Communities and International Policy Coordination." *International Organization* 46 (Winter): 1–35.

Hall, Peter A. 1997. "The Comparative Political Economy of Europe in an Era of Interdependence." In *Continuity and Change in Contemporary Capitalism,* edited by H. Kitschelt, P. Lange, G. Marks, and J. D. Stephens. Cambridge University Press (forthcoming).

Hamilton, Carl B., Ulf Jakobsson, Lars Jonung, Nils Lundgren, and Niels Thygesen. 1996. "Swedish Strategies at the European Union Intergovernmental Conference." SNS Occasional Paper. Stockholm (March).

Hancke, Bob, and David Soskice. 1996. "Coordination and Restructuring of Large French Firms: The Evolution of French Industry in the 1980s." Discussion Paper 96-303. Berlin: WZB.

Hatzius, Jan. 1994. "The Unemployment and Earning Effects of German Immigration."

Henning, Randall C. 1994. *Currencies and Politics in the United States, Germany and Japan.* Washington, D.C.: Institute for International Economics.

___. 1996. "Europe's Monetary Union and the United States." *Foreign Policy* 102 (Spring): 83–100.

Herrigel, Gary. 1993. "Large Firms, Small Firms and the Governance of Flexible Specialization: The Case of Baden-Wurttemberg and Socialized Risk." In *Country Competitiveness: Technology and the Organization of Work*, edited by B. Kogut. Oxford University Press.

Hill, John K, and José A. Mendez. 1984. "The Effects of Commercial Policy on International Migration Flows: The Case of United States and Mexico." *Journal of International Economics* 17 (August): 41–53.

Hoekman, Bernard, and Simon Djankov. 1996. "Catching up with Eastern Europe? The European Union's Mediterranean Free Trade Initiative." *World Economy* 19: 287–406.

Hollingsworth, J. Rogers, Philippe C. Schmitter, and Wolfgang Streeck, eds. 1994. *Governing Capitalist Economies: Performance and Control of Economic Sectors*. Oxford University Press.

Holtham, G., and Andrew J. Hughes-Hallett. 1987. "International Policy Cooperation and Model Uncertainty." In *Global Macroeconomic Policy: Conflict and Cooperation*, edited by Ralph C. Bryant and Richard Portes. London: Macmillan.

Horne, Jocelyn, and Paul Masson. 1988. "Scope and Limits of International Economic Cooperation and Policy Coordination." *IMF Staff Papers* 35: 259–96.

Ikenberry, G. John. 1993. "The Political Economy of Bretton Woods." In *A Retrospective on the Bretton Woods System*, edited by Michael D. Bordo and Barry Eichengreen, 155–99. University of Chicago Press.

Kenen, Peter B. 1990. "The Coordination of Macroeconomic Policies." In *International Policy Coordination and Exchange Rate Fluctuations*, edited by William Branson, Jacob A. Frenkel, and Morris Goldstein, 63–102. University of Chicago Press.

___. 1995. *Economic and Monetary Union in Europe: Moving beyond Maastricht*. Cambridge University Press.

Keohane, Robert. 1983. *After Hegemony*. Princeton University Press.

Kitschelt, Herbert. 1991. "Industrial Governance, Innovation Strategies, and the Case of Japan: Sectoral or Cross-National Analysis?" *International Organization* 45 (Autumn): 453–93.

Kreps, David. 1993. "Corporate Culture and Economic Theory." In *Perspectives on Positive Political Economy*, edited by James E. Alt and Kenneth A. Shepsle. Cambridge University Press.

Lehrer, Mark. 1996. "The German Model of Industrial Strategy in Turbulence: Corporate Governance and Managerial Hierarchies in Lufthansa." Discussion Paper 96-307. Berlin: WZB.

Lutz, Suzanne. 1993. *Die Steuerung industrieller Forschungskooperation.* Frankfurt/Main: Campus.

Morrow, James D. 1994. "Modeling the Forms of International Cooperation: Distribution versus Information." *International Organization* 48 (Summer): 387–423.

Muhleisen, Martin, and Klaus F. Zimmermann. 1994. "A Panel Analysis of Job Changes and Unemployment." *European Economic Review* 38 (April): 793–801.

Organization for Economic Cooperation and Development (OECD). 1994. *Vocational Training in Germany: Modernisation and Responsiveness.* Paris: OECD.

_____. 1995. *The OECD Jobs Study.* Paris: OECD.

Owen Smith, Eric. 1994. *The German Economy.* London: Routledge.

Patterson, Gardner. 1966. *Discrimination in International Trade: The Policy Issues, 1945–1965.* Princeton University Press.

Porter, Michael E. 1990. *The Competitive Advantage of Nations.* New York: Free Press.

Putnam, Robert, and Nicholas Bayne. 1987. *Hanging Together: Cooperation and Conflict in the Seven Power Summits.* Rev. ed. Harvard University Press.

Razin, Assef, and Efraim Sadka. 1995. *Population Economics.* Cambridge, Mass.: MIT Press.

Regini, Marino. 1995. *Uncertain Boundaries: The Social and Political Construction of European Economies.* Cambridge University Press.

Schmidt, Christoph M., Anette Gehrig Stilz, and Klaus F. Zimmermann. 1994. "Mass Migrations, Unions and Fiscal Migration Policy." *Journal of Public Economics* 55: 185–210.

Schoorl, Evert. 1995. "Working Party Three and the Dollar, 1961–1964." University of Groningen.

Schott, Jeffrey J. 1994. *The Uruguay Round: An Assessment.* Washington, D.C.: Institute for International Economics.

_____. 1995. "Reflections on TAFTA." In *Open for Business: Creating a Transatlantic Marketplace,* edited by Bruce Stokes. New York: Council on Foreign Relations.

_____. ed. 1996. *The World Trading System: Challenges Ahead.* Washington, D.C.: Institute for International Economics.

SOPEMI. 1995. *Trends in International Migration.* Annual Report. Paris: OECD.

Sorge, Arndt, and Malcolm Warner. 1987. *Comparative Factory Organization: An Anglo-German Comparison of Manpower in Manufacturing.* Aldershot, United Kingdom: Gower.

Soskice, David. 1990. "Reinterpreting Corporatism and Explaining Unemployment: Coordinated and Uncoordinated Market Economies." In *Labour Relations and Economic Performance*, edited by Renato Brunetta. London: Macmillan.

___. 1994. "Reconciling Markets and Institutions: The German Apprenticeship System." In *Training and the Private Sector: International Comparisons*, edited by Lisa M. Lynch. University of Chicago Press.

___. 1997. "Divergent Production Regimes. Coordinated and Uncoordinated Market Economies in the 1980s and 1990s." In *Continuity and Change in Contemporary Capitalism*, edited by H. Kitschelt, P. Lange, G. Marks, and J. D. Stephens. Cambridge University Press (forthcoming).

Stanton, Russell S., and Michael Teitelbaum. 1992. "International Migration and International Trade." Discussion Paper 160. Washington, D.C.: World Bank.

Streeck, Wolfgang, and others. 1987. *The Role of the Social Partners in Vocational Training in Germany*. Berlin: CEDEFOP.

Turner, Lowell. 1991. *Democracy at Work: Changing World Markets and the Future of Labor Unions*. Cornell University Press.

Vitols, Sigurt. 1995. "German Banks and the Modernization of the Small Firm Sector: Long-Term Finance in Comparative Perspective." Discussion Paper 95-309. Berlin: WZB.

Volcker, Paul. 1995. "The Quest for Exchange Rate Stability: Real or Quixotic?" London School of Economics.

Williamson, John. 1985. "The Exchange Rate System." Policy Analyses in International Economics no. 5. Rev. Washington, D.C.: Institute of International Economics.

Williamson, Oliver. 1985. *Institutions of Capitalism*. New York: Free Press.

Wilson, John S. 1996. "Eliminating Barriers to Trade in Telecommunications and Information Technology Goods and Services: Next Steps in Multilateral and Regional Liberalization Efforts." Washington, D.C.: International Technology Industry Council.

Winkelman, Rainer, and Klaus F. Zimmermann. 1993. "Aging, Migration and Labour Mobility." In *Labour Markets in an Aging Europe*, edited by P. Johnson and Klaus F. Zimmermann. Cambridge University Press.

Woolcock, Stephen. 1991. *Market Access Issues in EC-U.S. Relations: Trading Partners or Trading Blows*. London: Royal Institute of International Affairs.

___. 1996a. "European and North American Approaches to Regulation: Continued Divergence?" In *The End of the West*, edited by W. Wallace.

___. 1996b. "Strengthening EU-U.S. Commercial Relations?" LSE Centre for Research on the U.S.A., London School of Economics.

Working Party 3. 1966. *The Balance of Payments Adjustment Process.* Washington, D.C.: OECD.

World Bank. 1990. *World Development Report.* Oxford University Press.

Wyplosz, Charles. 1996. "An EMS for Both Ins and Outs." Graduate Institute of International Studies, University of Geneva.

Zimmermann, Klaus F. 1995a. "European Migration: Push and Pull." *Annual Bank Conference on Development Economics.* Washington, D.C.: World Bank.

___. 1995b. "Tackling the European Migration Problem." *Journal of Economic Perspectives* 9 (2): 45–62.

Zweimuller, Josef, and Rudolf Winter-Ebmer. 1996. "Immigration, Trade and Austrian Unemployment." Discussion Paper 1346. London: Centre for Economic Policy Research.

About the Authors

Barry Eichengreen is John L. Simpson Professor of Economics and Professor of Political Science at the University of California, Berkeley.

Riccardo Faini is Professor of Economics at the University of Brescia, Italy.

Fabio Ghironi is a Ph.D. candidate in economics at the University of California, Berkeley.

Jeffrey Schott is Senior Fellow at the Institute for International Economics, Washington, D.C.

David Soskice is Director of the the Research Institute for Employment and Economic Change at the Social Science Research Center, Berlin, and Emeritus Fellow of University College, Oxford University.